For questions contact: greenethisdesert@gmail.com
Instagram: jamesryangreene

ISBN: 978-1-7332068-0-8 (print)

Cover Drawing: Rachel Rodriguez
Instagram: Raemelina.art
Raemelina.art@gmail.com

Cover Design: A. Cuozzo

Back Cover Photo: Amber de Giorgio

First Printing, 2019
Printed in the United States of America

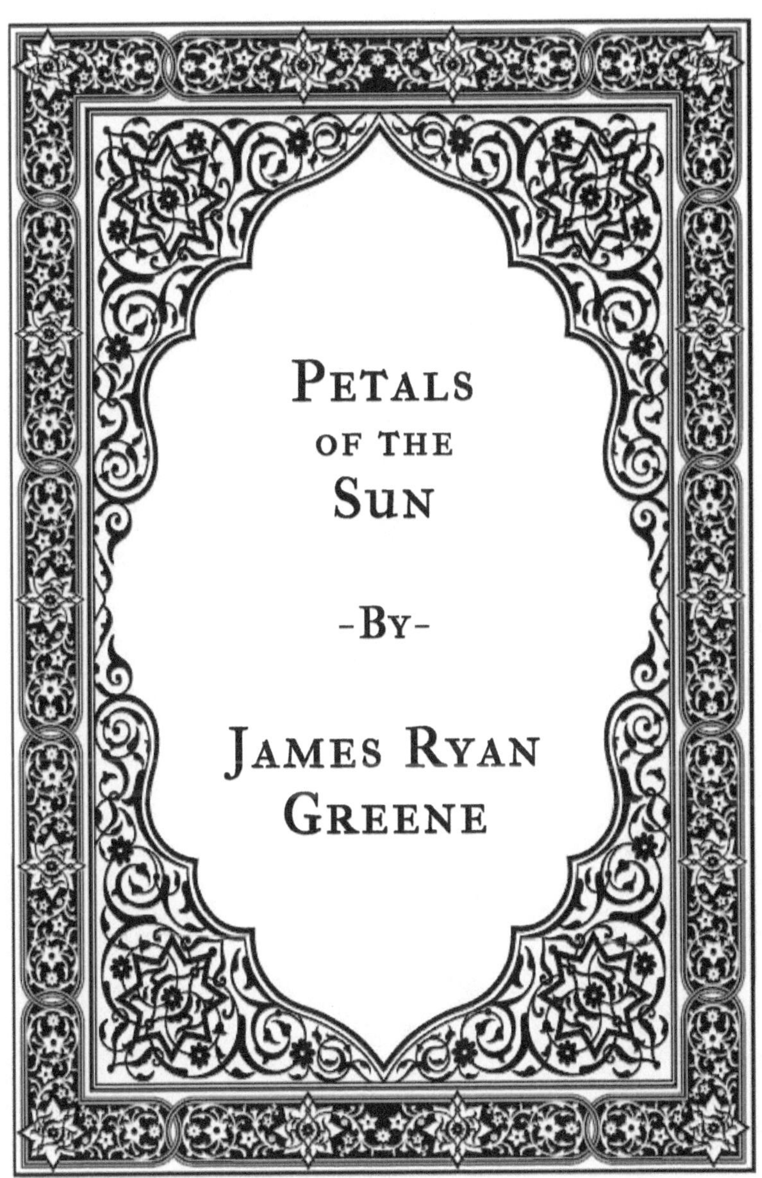

Petals of the Sun

-By-

James Ryan Greene

TABLE OF CONTENTS

PART I

PART II

Part III

Part IV

PART V

PART VI

Introduction

These are my lyrical excursions through words in verses;
This is an ongoing self-discovery formed from:
prayers & most persistent longings;
elegies for the martyred parts of me
that had to be sacrificed in the flux of Becoming;
artifacts from a rhythmic inquiry of Being;
impressions left from the edge of my perception;
notes to self from encounters with the Moment;
love letters to the Earth;
and monuments my mind makes
in the midst of tumult & silence.
These are my offerings
of song.

"Is it true Prince, that you once said **'beauty' will save the world**? *Gentleman," he cried loudly to them all, "the prince insists that beauty will save the world! And I insist that he has such playful thoughts because he's in love now."*

-Fyodor Dostoevsky, in **The Idiot-**

PART I

Opening Invocation

Apollo I call upon thee
To lend the light of thy *logos* to my songs;
If even only to hold just one
Petal of the Sun

If language be the compromise
Just short of silence
Let my words
Accommodate the transcendent
But not cast aspersions on the world

If silence be the limit
Let my words approach it
Yea, let them exceed it!
Each inflection with untrammeled abandon
A brief intimation of Heaven

An oracular utterance
Containing truth without
Gracelessly revealing it
For truth has not run out

A way to paint the negative space
That we may apprehend
Even just a shadow of it
Partly revealed; a portal opened
The sketch of an echo

Guide aright
The aim of my arrow
Lest I become unintelligible
Let there be no distance
Between my word and my soul

Dionysus I call upon thee, too
To lend the shadow of thy *eros* to my songs;
If even only to hold just one
Petal of the Sun

ALL THAT I AM

"The winds of God's Grace are always blowing,
it is for us to raise our sails."
-Sri Ramakrishna-

All that I am has been given to the wind
I have set sail upon this oceanic feeling
Like a tide that knows no shore
For I am but a ripple
In the wake of Thy grace

And I must've been swung
From the furthest star
Through the heights of heaven
Where time cannot touch
And gravity cannot reach

Between breaths is the unbroken knowing:
All that I am is all that You have given
And what more could be asked for?
When the road narrows
I shall take with me
Only what I can carry
But Your love I will keep
So very near to me
And all else will be
For the wind's taking

Fleeting Farwell
-To a Brother-

It always is a fleeting farewell
What the wind takes with it
But I'm as sure as
The times we've shared in starlight
That in seasons soon to bloom
We will become what we beheld

Our love is a turning leaf
With colors yet to be seen
And the sweet fruit that together we tasted
Will again, in a day unbeknownst,
Be on a branch within reach

As what's wild would
In our separate peace
It must move with mystery
But every thought and heartspark
Shall keep the torch alight
The one set afire
With our ancient flame
It will always stay the same

Our kinship has shown me
The golden that hides in the dark wood's grain,
And opened eyes able to shine
With loves all-permeating gaze
Penetrating the thickest shade
Persisting through the many roles
That we both have played

And given community to a lone boy
Amidst a world of those

Hidden behind the fence
And inspired me to become my utmost self
And for this I am eternally grateful

I Heard From the World

I heard from the world:
That our exile began at birth
Gripped within the struggle between
Destruction and creation,
That all we encounter
On this side of the veil
Shall take us away from spirit,
That through our choices we may move
Toward animal or angel

I heard from the world:
That one must stand and take
The arrows of guilt and shame
So unconsciously cast
O the endless crucifixions
Of a herd-like morality
So slavishly obeyed

I heard from the world:
This paradigm of paradox
That we have been casted into
Is but a house of mirrors
And every reflection shall help us find
Our blindspots

I heard from the world:
To take chance by the hand
And make this a dance
Thus you may enter the house of cards
But it all may fall from just the gust of a butterfly's wing
So I knocked a simple rhythm and gained admission
To gather the inheritance
That God has bequeathed me

I heard from the world:
And yet, even now
I gamble my fate
Into the hands of the divine force
That will send me along a wild course
For the lion does not touch
The true heir

I heard from the world:
That I've been suffocating to breath,
I've been blinded to see
That what the wind takes with it
Is what I no longer need
And the mountain must crack open
For the springs of truth
To surface like bolts from the blue

I heard from the world:
And still I will
Look out into this world
With all the light of my eye
And find reflected the charge of God's grandeur
Manifest in the continuous stream of miracles
And answered prayers
Which comprise our daily life

(What inconceivable skill it must take
To strike this fine balance
Between form and formless
To make what appears to be two out of one
To keep the stars apart!)

SELF-FULFILLING PROPHECY

This life is a self-fulfilling prophecy
Of fickle fates that dare to be destiny
Of flight paths that land on the lip of insanity
And you are as immaculate as the autumnal leaf
Whose fall is a flawless, divinely orchestrated feat

This life is a self-fulfilling prophecy
We are free to be as we dream
Therein we create the meaning
From castles of dust,
Forests made of mist,
Mountains made of cloud:
Call it what you will
But what we choose to see
Is often a projection of our own belief

And the power of suggestion
Has us following the words that the charlatans speak
Searching outside of our Selves for a guarantee
And with our infinite creative potential
We unconsciously manifest realities
Then, silently, they are taken on as an identity
(we were born with the keys to the kingdom
but who's been looking after them?)

The future is a premonition
Which we are slowly remembering
And the consummation of thy vision lies within
But only a soft feather can cut
Through the veil of forgetfulness to see that
You are home from all your restless seeking
Feel at the center of your being
A sanctuary that's unwavering

Beyond the reaches of this world
Untouched by the tides of time
You've been dying to live
Just breathe in and you are born again
You are already free
This consecration you've been craving
Is a harvest that's ripened from within

You are your own gift,
Which awaits to be unwrapped
That which was, is and always will be
That which the sun has sung into being
With a cry of light, a breath blown through the bones
And an eye to emanate God's illumination
Like a star that carries forth the light of heaven
And blood is thus kindled beneath flesh
Quickened by the same force that flies the planets

This life is a self-fulfilling prophecy
And your soul is the song
That God is eternally singing

In My Time

My allegiance is to the stars;
My homage for the earth
And the wanderings shall
Weave into synchronicity;
The journeywork shall be dispersed!

I need ample space for my meandering
When moments of madness
Parlay to sweet ecstasy
It is not one or the other
That leaves nothing in between

The circle remains unbroken within me
Yet never too far gone for cordiality
It is not all or nothing
That leaves us thrashing to extremes
In the bittersweet dance of polarity

There's a serpent climbing my spine
And I will answer the call of the divine
Like Spring answers the Sun's invocation
With flowers as the sacramental offering
And luminescent eyes whence the inner sanctum casts light

I will vanquish odds with this alliance
Armed to the heart with these flowers
Constellations to wreathe my crown
In my own time I'll know the balance
Wandering earth in search of the middle ground

Searching for Words

Searching for words to convey
What no word can contain
Is like trying to catch the wind in a net,
Like trying to climb a mountainous cloud,
Like trying to hold the whole ocean in your hands

Such is the plight that love compels us to overcome:
To condense the limitless expanse of perception and feeling,
To breathe form out of the amorphous,
To fit the moon into a drop of dew
And translate the mountain spring into the open sea

It asks us to dare, like the flower that pushes up
Through the crack in the pavement,
Arising from the light of silence
To build an altar of beauty; an offering to all that is unsayable
A bridge back to blossomed consciousness
Parting the waters for the attainment of unity

Now you don't have to try and blow out the sun for anyone
This love is grandiose, but not delusional
And it would be impossible if we were not a miracle
When you give yourself to the process
It becomes a prayer that says itself
Like the fragrance of flowers: it comes forth of its own accord

Falling Petals

I have watched falling petals
Get hitched upon the wind
But I do not know
Where they fall:
The beauty of spring can be so prodigal

I have felt the ecstasy and misery of this existence
But I have begun to forget which ones which
For they give way to each other
As quick as a coin can flip
So I take respite from my fickle senses:
The freedom found in silence begets innocence

I have prayed my way
Into blessed redemption and beautiful ruin
Yet the mystery of each moment
Makes me surrender to Thy design:
For there is wonder in not knowing why

I have watched falling petals
Lift upon the wind
And where they fall I may never know
Perchance they will land at my feet:
Somewhere in between
Remembering and forgetting

Hallowed Isles
-In homage to Malta-

I gather myself
Between the breaking
Of island waves
In the flickered reflection
Of these waves

I was movement—
An Immaculate Happening,
A great exhalation
From the mouth of the wind,
A glimmer upon the face of the waters

Then, there comes over me
This ancient feeling
I get when glancing out
At these vast valleys
That give their song to the sea

Behold: the rock-lipped terraces,
Flat cascades, slowly rippling earth;
Scent of cypress & tender herbs
Lantana & Nasturtium
Flowing though stone

Whose life is this that I find entering my eyes?
Is all this blessedness my reflection?
I can only think to reciprocate by
Expanding the radius of my embrace
As far as my heart can handle

And in this way, weave coherence
Unto the chaos-laden reality

Such is the way of service:
Making sanctuary
Wherever you find yourself

And you can take it with you—
Along the waterfront
Outside the Old City's last bastions
Through the Hallowed Isles
And great Archipelagos of our Soul

* * *

PART II

Elemental Magic

The glimmer burst blazing lit
Tracing heavens arc
That all trees bend skyward to;
Rapt in the sun's cincture
The mystic assemblage bolt and bloom

Phantoms faring forth along ley lines
Burning spears needlecraft sown
Vials of life that rectify
Pent fire pillars of my soul

Feathered petals of lightwings
Seraph airborne lambency
Plying the welkin's wake
Such ethereal flight
Calibrates thine eye aloft

Breeze dashing quicksilver
Over star-glittered water
And it's this shine I take to
Catching glare on me

Apparitions in tow
Those moon-hitched, tryst-twined
Following with fluid step
Promises of rain that spread
Upon the anywhere yet

Sunsunken afterash leaving black
Of cloudpetals kindled
Eidolons blending crimson
By thus, roses are wreathed:
An inflorescent sky!

Midnight ebon raven and all the shadowplay
Labyrinthine cloudwork of thy glided escort
Fresh drifts, snow ghosts
Whose white weight furls into Springs

Elemental magic! this perennial miracle
Of hearts infusion, spirited to ignite
Native luster, pullulating seeds of light
What is this eluding essence
That forays into form?

I Will Make A Garden

I will make a garden of the foulest ground!
Suture the wound with vines
And suck the poison out
To alchemize an altar
For the seasons,
By death to renew

I will green deserts from their desiccation!
Conjure clouds with the sorcery of trees
And pull the arrows out
To ameliorate the earthen frame
For the seasons,
By death to renew

I will create the space
And have abundance become of it
To merge earthly substance
With cosmic force
For the seasons,
By death to renew

Aubade Prayer

Twilight precursor;
Some pillars of thy build-up!
Beams that precede
A forelighted likeness
Of the upcoming flooding
Thou orb of such effulgence
Bedash'd efflux from the infinite tessellation
Blossoming renewal with airy exclamation!

This I scale, with wings upraised
In the fervor glistening
Budding vernal my limbs
Swarming forested with green flame
Harbinger of ye scarlet heat
Flood me abundantly!
Come, come with thy finest gleam!
I will break my branches to bear this fruit for thee!

Plea to the Eve Lowering

Daylight my dying flare;
This plea to the eve lowering
These last beams I bask
With dusk and dew pooling
Yet for these fine shadings I pine
That careen through treetop interstice
Like ropes to rappel
Our descent into darkening

Let not these petals lock
To frost forgotten!
Dim not on my sight!
These eyes must dawn noctilucent
And lit by the fallen night
For to guide my gaze unwavering!
How else could I come back to thee?
Than with orbs of my own for lighted visioning!

Keepers of the Immortal Symmetry

If I were One of that age
When oaks castellated
Nature's ornate frame
And bison roamed majestic
No field left untrodden
By their brilliant march
When the hallowing was done
By the very dance that swept
Gigantic billows of cloud and smoke

If I were autochthon of that echelon
When oaks girded like castles
Keepers of the immortal symmetry
And owls were the only to pronounce
The lilted inscriptions of divinity…

I would be a fox
Mounting the steep escarpments
Amid hickory's flaking bark

I would be a falcon
Fled along the wax-melt lines
Of cloud and smoke
Dancing fire from twilit vapor
Catching a kiss
Before the parted lips
Have swallowed another sun for sleep

If I were a dawn unto that day,
The heartwood within concentric bark rings
I would sing with Mother Earth's hallowed spontaneity
And be a keeper of immortal symmetry

After a Burning

After a Burning
And the licking tongue of flames
Suture and assuage my fringes unkempt

The soothe of the Sun's second emanation!
Sweetspires that lick again
With an ardor unquenched

Blackened monuments!
Dead or alive, why trifle to distinguish?
Both being mutually inclusive and self-fulfilling

From what unlimited retention,
From what rimless brink,
Do you billow dimension and density?
To forms we oft' see as so empty
Thus to inflame…

A torch for perpetuity
A beacon to thwart the invasive torpor
Acedia taking no grasp in such light

And the rampant spread
Of a sacrificial regeneration
Catalyzed by a charred catharsis
Grants life anew!
With footholds for further growth
To continue our endless ascent
For future feet and ages hence
Cycling back enlivened…

A death for life to live for
A life for death to die for

Burning off old for the bud-swell of ripe

Before the Sun Climbs Dawn

Before the sun climbs dawn
And changes guard with the farther stars
We're being called

To be of the day's opening eye
In a most golden hour
When Gods breathe renewal into being

To alchemize the slumbered dream
With waking reality
And partake in the birthing of new worlds

O' to be of the lighted air!
And distillation of dews
Fleshing love into blood

When Heaven has wreathed the horizon
With an adorned display
As the sky is dyed such amazing shades

Show me the way and I will follow the flow of echoes
O' I can hear it now, the sound of subdued darkness
Gathered by God at dawn, as my prayers catch fire

As Prayers Catch Fire

I

I keep lighting
These prayers on fire
With the eternal flame of my soul
Sending scintillant smoke signals
From this side of the veil
Toward the One

I am the kindled wick
And the moth drawn to it
I am the countless thousand years
That culminates with Here
I am the ephemeral glimpse
Within the eternal gaze

You are the Truth
That I can't ignore
You are the long-awaited isle,
The signal from the shore
You are the paradox
That shows me who I am
By showing me who I am not

If I am nothing more
Than a cloud to add color
To your storm of light
Then it's just as well
For I am still yours

If I am nothing more
That a mote of dust
Suspended in your sunbeam

Then it's just as well
For I am still yours

If I am nothing more
Than a grain of sand
Upon your immortal shore
Then it's just as well
For I am still yours

For you are the flame that sets prayers ablaze,
The light that it gives off,
And the smoke signals that rise from thus

You shine the light of thy guidance
Through the fog of my confusion
And all that's left for me to do is trust

II

I don't wish to pretend to know anything
Other than my love for You

And through that I shall know everything
That I could ever need to

And through that I shall love everyone
Because they are me and we are You

When I use to say your name
I would speak it in a half-whipser
Instantly trembling at the connotations set forth

But now when I call upon your name,
Looking to the night sky with a head full of questions,
Watching the signal fires scintillate at the mention of your name,

I do so knowing that this moment contains
The bounty of eternity,
Knowing that your name brings Us closer,
Knowing that your name is the gateway to a larger place,
That it ferries me from busy harbors
That, in saying your name, I forget my own

I Wonder

I wonder in what language do Angels speak?
And does it does it sound
Like flowers endlessly opening?

That voice in the sky we call the wind,
Could it be them?
I wonder where does the wind begin?
And does it rush from their wingtips?

And that voice in my mind I call "Me",
Could that be a wayward whisper
That got past the gates of eternity?

THAT KIND OF SILENCE

I'm always craving that kind of silence
Where one can hear
Wings part the breeze
And the bloom and burst
Of clouds changing form
And the flicker and fade,
The far-off music of the stars

In this timeless stillness—I ripen
Up out of the coffins of my concepts—I lift

I'm always craving that thing beyond naming
Which is within us, always waiting
Which is without us,
Transfixing attention in aesthetic arrest
When our world is lit with new colors
You, whose essence cannot be captured,
Whom I seek insatiably

Speak to me if You will, in Your thousand wordless verses
And I shall go roaming in the stillness

THRONE OF THIS MOMENT

I ask not for heaven or hell
Nor for anything other than
This moment that stands before me
In all its awfully terrific, grandiose glory

This moment: the constant culmination of creation,
Of your place in space;
I gladly take a seat on this throne
For there is no difference
Between you and the sun
That sits on a golden horizon

I ask to be cleansed of my subjective preferences
That keep me locked in exclusivity
And makes life like a ripple in reverse,
Tightening circles till only I am the center of my narcissism

This endless list of likes and dislikes
That you call your personality
That you claim as your identity
Only serves to box you into bias

May I no longer behave like a prodigal son
Squandering my heaven-sent inheritance
Running about for the party that's always elsewhere
With all the subtle ways we summon an escape plan
As if we should be transported from this place
Taunted by some mirage, tricked by some façade

Let us consecrate the hour!
Let us take a cosmic course toward a universal season!
Let thy vanities be stripped away
In the effacement & lucidity of numinous truth

CASTING QUALITIES

I find it interesting
How we call this person or that thing *sacred*
Whens Gods divine involvement is especially evident

But what of those dimly lit places,
Or those of us who commit unthinkable acts?
There, is God withdrawn? Shall we forego homage?

You see, this business of assigning qualities
is like trying to divide the sky:
The vast expanse of His being flows unbroken through
everything
There is nowhere that he is not, nowhere outside of his purview

Often, with our words, we create a cage
And its like trying to catch the wind in a butterfly net
Trying to map vast continents on a postage stamp

Is God not also the flower that can bloom through the night?
That can bloom underground?
That can bloom inside out?

What if, instead of just praising those things we find pleasing
We offered uplifting words to those things
That challenge our sense of symmetry,
That push against the limits of our definitions

Who knows, they might be like the island that was risen into a
mountain
It would be like kissing someone's wound
Instead of salting it with insults & desecrating language

APHORISMS

Objects await
For the meaning we make

Meanings gather momentum
And take us with them

The past is alive
Within our present perception

Reality takes form
Around our words

The ego sticks to the story,
The soul plays in the immediate presence

Our choices — that's all
We can ever hope to own

Time is what we are given
And the forms thereof — they will always decay

Reach not
For the fruits of your doing

Those are the seeds
That God shall reap

All we must do is trust the field
in which He shall sow

* * *

When I can see the same "I" in every other,
Then I'll know I have done my work

When I see my own body when I look upon the Earth,
Then I'll know I have done my work

And when I can see the work of ego
As the play of consciousness
Then I can
Just be

* * *

How you relate to the present moment
Is how you relate to your Soul
Is how you relate to God

If your ability to love yourself
Is contingent upon achievements
Then the world has set the terms
For your most sacred relationship

If your conception of spiritual living
Is limited to rigid practices or substances
Then religion and infatuation has come between
That most beautiful relationship of yourself and God

* * *

Be where you are
Look where you haven't seen
Find what you perceived to be missing

Build upon the silence
Lest you take away from it

Now is the choice you're always making
And you have no choice in making it

* * *

There has been too much emphasis
Placed upon answers
When questions are the compass
And it's what we don't know
That creates the space
For Wonder to roam
Like the silence between notes
That gives rise to a musical flow

* * *

O the endless crucifixions!
Someone forgot to say you don't have to partake
In the unconscious game of projecting shame
To externalize the corner of hell that you've been occupying
Who is this tyrant inside
With dictates always verging on fascism?

When you find yourself attempting to superimpose
The insular findings of your unique path onto others
Then you're walking a tightrope:
To report your findings is necessary
But to prescribe them as the one and only way,
That's when we verge upon fascism

The temptation of ideology
Lies in the power that it bestows
The power built up by
The pillars of people's belief
The power of certainty when we supply

A presupposed answer to everything

* * *

Is it that God is of our own making?
A way to relate to the ultimate and inconceivable
Is it that we are always chasing that which is inescapably true?
Is God our fumbling intimation of what we perceive as
inescapably true?

Or is God a feeling?
A level of reality spoken only by eyes
To be entered by way of the sound of a stream
A territory to inhabit, a journey you can always start
From wherever you are

Or is it the plenum of the senses?
Surely God is an experience
And religion is the response to it

* * *

And what is happiness? But a curious boundlessness, into which
we may never arrive, but are endlessly lured unto through our
questions thereof, through conceiving of it as a destination to be
discovered. Would we really want to arrive there though?
Would we want to exist in that impossible state of zero tension?
Or would it be more to the point to desire an optimal meaning
for our suffering? For the tension to be felt as that of a bow
quivering with an aimed arrow? Or as Rilke says, "…as the
arrow endures the bowstrings tension, so that gathered in the
snap of its release, it can be more than itself."

* * *

And no matter what it seems that the dancing coquetry of opposites will, when taken in with a sweeping glance, coalesce into a unity of events, which appears to us as a narrative of commendable coherence that deserves to be met with gratitude. But, in the midst of this drama so full of dread, one cant help but feel thoroughly aimless, without compass, a fragmented infinity unhinged into temporality. Then a mythic potential calls forth from us a certain elusive, wild vigor that has the overpowering abundance of our heart flow into the future, despite the suspicion that an *enantiodromia* is likely looming on our life's horizon. Life longs to give us a new page; or, life longs to give us the thrust to make it to the opposite page by way of a revolving door.

* * *

I've made so many mistakes, but I am learning to love those times: it's like loving when flowers die, for that too is a time to be celebrated. And you must know that the flowers of the spring are very dear to me. But, destruction is the prerequisite act of creation; this grand project we call our life is subject to endless revisions. Many petals must fall as we try "to invent new flowers."

* * *

The waters that gather, and the animals: they live in something akin to a state of grace; their instincts opened wholly toward life, their certain death unbeknownst to them. But we, in which dwells the great dread of death, make every conceivable leap toward some beyond, and then wonder why the instincts go awry and the senses atrophy. Then we, the ones with such sophisticated civility and morality, must fumble about in a quest for our grace. Hafiz chimes in and reminds me, however, "to deeply compute the impossibility that there is anything else but grace."

* * *

How do we speak of the limitations of the ego without denigrating it? We are builders of our life, and the ego is a positively crucial tool. Out of zealotry, we may fancy to disparage the little self, with our eye to the great beyond, the soul, the Self. But how could we curse the ground we stand on? Wouldn't that be a divine irony: formulating negations of the ego with the very apparatus and lens itself. It's as if we stand upon a mountain's focal point that just peeks out of the waters to form an island, and then in naiveté try to postulate that the only thing that matters is the parts of the mountain that are submerged and hence less visible.

* * *

All this time spent in the shade, and to think: I've been sitting under a fruit tree.

* * *

A song is that vessel which catches our heart's blossoming overabundance; a mirror to reflect our spirits effulgence in a moment of fullness; existing somewhere in between a premonition and a memory, where meanings intersect and a temple is erected—that's a song.

* * *

Part III

Autumnal Ode

Autumnal tints whispering sway
And the bare-branch-chatter
Sounds upon the air
Voicing stirred depth hints
Of sycamores white-crowned counsel

Inhales: taking to smoke and flame
Breathe: so the fire swings, its flavor in me
Letting the cinder sink in and sear…
And the herbage is sweet!
A tinder transcendent, for the bosom pulsant

How many a wane and retrograde
Of the moon's one-eyed noctilucence
Fused – the mystical synthesis
And paraselene encircling
Caresses earth's curves, it returns

Fighting animals intone frenzied ferocity
Through the twisted hedgerow
The rip-tooth of jagged rungs and splinter-scythe
Till a body goes down, crowded out
Away through crisped leaves stealing

O' the seminal dividends of this moment hearken'd!
Life everlasting inviolate from times lapsing
From the siphon'd wellsprings
O' It's more than I've ever been told!
Prodigal, more than its weight in gold

The wild grass catching seed
Going for the sky
As scattered ashes, stars shot over me

Folding back into eternity
From a one-eyed brief wink

Sidereal rhythms flecked unto night skies
Inflections of the corporeal life

Seeding the Sundream

I

Winged sun path: mining the fertile veins of space
Great chariot of fire and the monarch throne
His furrows dawn-laced
Of what consummate flight
Of what broad swath he cuts
His cycles wide sweep

Striking free a prayer paean
On her horizon-alter
Carillon sky wind (unfettered by somatic structure)
Chants o' life eternal – enamored!
With an ephemeral mandala of vanishing etherics

A heaved disk of infinity condensed; soared oneiric
Celestial host of archangelic helm
Across the planes, only to translate
As pure, golden light

O' magic-emblazoned mind, us riders of the fine line
Drunken liquescence, dreaming dizzy sunlight
While backdrops brushed saffron from azure overarch
The firebrands-iridescent scatter
Through prisms, between gossamer
Where waters caustic drop melts the stones alluvium

Solar spills sinuous flood
Of fountainhead-fed mouth
Love wrote out in fleeting adorations
By star-born supplication

II

O' horizon's crepuscular headdress!
Blushes bloom a plumed crest
From her spangled commissure
The distant vistas adorned!
With glided silvery spindrifts
The violets swirl to sapphire undulant

Night quickly grabbing after; their immortal chase
To seal the seams of the fourth horizon
And we still dancing!
Across tightropes, those diaphanous beams
As hands about a guitar
The pattern-woven strings
Skies scraped by sicklesmoon's subtle creep
How I too am clawing for the sky's keep!

Soul Course: if only to give,
For this woodland depth
And verdant leaflet,
My entirety–
Then have all of me!

Taproot reach lowly!
All your puissance
To the aquifer and sodden mineral trace
Breathe! The depth of ages elapsed
Pioneer tree brave blind height!
Hardy on the cold, exposed plain

Star dial set to tomorrow, a domain sacrosanct
Renascent with the feral earth, she my uttermost
And I: seeding the sundream, from the wooded wild autumnal!

SAFE WITH ME

Your neurodiversity is safe with me
Like the hummingbird's tongue
Made psychoactive, fermented by the
Honey turning into mead

I do my best to keep both feet on the ground
With these frenetic synergies enacted within me
No longer do the bricks stay upon one another
Since I see your loaded gun
Pointed at everything

I wont look on with scorn though
At what you're settling for,
That which takes not long to seek
A well-paved pathway, there's nothing to fill the empty
Lobotomized by the Western conditioning

There are a million minor melodramas
To postpone the problem
Bought and sold obscenities
To keep us from facing the deeper thirst
That has gone for ages without slaking

Turn your back on the culture!
The broken system is breaking us!
There's something else filling those
Of inner wealth and plumbed depth
Who open the window to the rarefied breeze

And so to forest I shall return!
To be of Gaian mind
And embed within a larger cohesion
To let loose in the landscape

My long-pent, shallowed breathing

Soundtrack Unsung

As if the soundtrack were unsung
By the daylong lachrymal misting
I labor over the notes of some knell
To what, extend the drenching?

Am I the last to know?
Now that fever pitch is reached
This would have to be
The most beautifully awful, grandiose joke
To have ever jeered at a sentient being

I wont say an easy cliché
But what's most bedeviling —
We've arrived at the unsplittable particle
When Eden has seen unprecedented spoiling

I was the lost hologram;
The dream was lost on me
Then I had a divine scream sweep through
My pretended arrangements
And dismantle the juxtaposition
Of façade and mirage
Till naught was left but a column of light
And a passage of unrehearsed happening

And since: my swim is not sped
By the wake behind me
Nor the wings flown by the air
Through which I'm flying
The oak to an iris
Is a flower just as fleet

An Ocean Becometh
(The Revolution Everywhere)

Of the echoes leapt up in me
This river kept pent
The hungers gnaw and surged flood
A mountain beneath the sea
Pulsant to the weir and riparian
Hastened flow, my swelling tides

Of all the dreams that didn't stick
Transient flickers, always racing sundown to get
Too green to burn though! With forest floor soddenness
Dauntless as any earth, and terra-forming internal
Gold in the hands of the wise
Palpitant with this my bosom imbibes

The revolution everywhere!
Nameless movement afoot
As the wounds run deeper
Scabbing up and healing inward
To grow from within!
Endogenous; cracking up through pavement

The carapace transcended!
More than the sum of our afflictions (that displaced weight)
Flown not only by freshet! Thy reservoir unsheathed
Emergent with the wishes
Left in the fountain
With the rusted mint hidden

The revolution everywhere!
An ocean becometh
Of all our one-drop, insular dreaming
Seaward ever-bent the yearned for union

And like continental drift
Making mountains illimitable, the throb tectonic

An ocean becometh
Of the tumid tides
Brimming high banks
And dammed up outcries
The spring lines created
Whence we shine

A stand in the riparian
Who are the buffers between
Manning the high spate
Wading in the fire unseen
Incised meander where the waters wore course
Tattoos of the thunder-thrust
Lichen of the cemetery stones
Where only the ghosts come and go
Migrants of the cycling tornadic
To find the vernal eye

Grape vine take hold! Pull apart this many-times-mended fence
Bleed into one! Embryo to be birthed
Flash together! On the windfall into landslide
Melody roam free! Eclogue and the poetic dialect
Sun streaks thread unto me!
Assemble the flowers, of thus I dream

O' Pariah! Our long-awaited isle
Lending breath amid perilous
Coming of season from delitescence
Organic breath, your pollen dehisced
Set free from the plagued tyranny
Bearing flowers at sea, of thus I dream

Together we can reconnect the tatters
And threadbare isle of thee I
For the mergence and joined fray, crossing diluvial divide
Continued kisses and constant harmony
Only handshakes away
The unfurling inflorescence, of thus I dream

Far Walks

I

Far Walks
In a far, far forest flown
Forward ever further
With the balance that's found by motion
As a bicycle rides to stay upright
Volitant: a moving meditation

I keep my eye to the trees
For to charm my sight
That it may spur my flight
O how they are always reaching spiralwise!

Their levity pays no mind to gravity
By worship of the sun
Their crowns take a swirling pursuit
Galaxies unsheathed from a seed
With the wildest seeds yet to be sown
Gambling chance by the lightning bolt's hand

Nowhere is there to go
Other than where the trees point
The love without end;
Their abundance cannot be bankrupted
Not merely statues; it works as it's dreamt
In dream-motion

Far Walks!
Till there are enough trees
Between me and the city
(But who's been breathing you?
And was it a deeper breath we drew?)

II

Nightwatch of the woodline
And I have endeavored to the furthest fathom
Seen my enamored rambling through
Into the velvet evening
My fires doused out by the sodden dew

But why is it only when
You are deep in the pockets,
And fringing at loose ends,
The heart has you ever onward?
O' the hastening hunger!
More than just animals to be hunted!

While moonclouds were on the sail
Showing bone-smooth, the beams
Shining like a glassy sea
Loading night to the hills
Shadows teeming to the hilt

And in just a blink evening grew dark,
I find myself searching through midnights
Elusive lucidity, serpent charming
The coiled emotions and hurt from its hiding
The billows of my smoking breath

Chewing on the roots to get to the truth
And there's been magic made afoot
On the Nightwatch, till I have seen meaning
If not by the color of the bark
Then surely by the shape of the leaves
Looking yonder unto Heaven's tallest vault

III

It could be that I live within myths
Swinging upon windward gossamer
And other such motes of dust
That would otherwise go unseen
If not for an incident of sun
That peeks through the temporal aperture

Here I hover behind the sky
Where there always lurks a shadow
That knows no quenching
If not for a swallowed sun

Now it is all I can do
To live in agreement
With the cycles of the moon
In nocturnes: a shapeshifter,
A chameleon amid mandalas—Of forest gardens!
Traipsing about the sunlit heights—Of wild walks!
Free flowing the full length of my being
O' the amaranthine processions of sky
O' the blossoming velocity!

I'm going to float out the window
And just see what happens
Perchance to bring forth the parts of me
Yet to be born
The truth of which
Lies somewhere in between

So I see the forest from the trees
Way out in the great elsewhere
Forging the unknown, running the edges, seeking the obscurity
Playing in the liminal space

At the very stabbing tip of the spearhead of existence
Bleeding from the lesion that lets enter cosmic providence
Where futures, worlds, and astral probabilities are pioneered
Where the voice you sing is allowed the latitudes to play the
breeze
Where I can hear the silence that brings the soul out of hiding
Where I can see the darkness that shows
The inner eye it's lighting
Where I can draw upon a deeper breath
Where I can breach the firewall of my fears most nightmarish
Where I can come out of the eclipsing cloud
Where I can uncap my glacial veins and let the mountains out!
Where I can find the fringing outer reaches
That outfit your eye to find gemstones in common sights
And gather poetry from the branches of a ripened life

Ropewalker with one foot ever further:
Cast off the mummy-wrappings of this temporal life!
Tend inward—it's the window into the now!
Dive in with the teardrops!
Escape through the cracks in the façade!
Dance upon the serpent's head!
For we are precariously placed,
Balanced wide over the deepest grave;
No! Don't leave your love
Locked inside the Mother Earth
Bring it out with flowers
No! Don't leave your love
Locked inside your heart
Bring it out with laughter
O' the sunlit heights you may know!
When you leave the trees
To leap greenly unto a new spring

And when I've gone windward

In this dreaming direction
Within the sun's scope
O I swear I'm ecstatic!
Escorted out of the cadaver (my mortal cavern)
Into the sunlit heights
And I shall live my life as a tree that offers fruit
Onto the alter of the ether!

Lightbird

I

I am a lightbird cast skyward
Into heavenly processions of smoke and fire
Living by the breezes, ascending on celestial seasons
Soaring into mornings, fast as a flying arrow
I dodge lightning bolts all the while
I've been getting my wings one feather at a time
In all this longing for the sky

O tell me of the sky's cycles!
Enough of this living life in the rearview
Scorned with a shoe-gaze
Staring into the entangling material world
I will look only to the heavens and their turnings

This is the astral passage
Hitched upon the chariot Sun
Out of this mazework
Of endless matter
Onward the star-distance
Into the broad halls of eternity
— Immortalization!

But save for me some degree of mystery!
Just enough to set forth
An unquenchable curiosity
A lust to implore the flickering flame
- That my compass shall always be hung
Upon this everlasting lantern
—Imperishable!

A sacred & secret road

Edified with a living light
Where no dust hath settled
The vistas open up
Into eternal deeps
Lit with the greatest of emanations
At the end of this world

II

Breath of flower; Flesh of fruit
I am hearing blossoms
In a poetic reverie
Perpetually lifted
By thus perfumed

These thoughts, to my mind are crowned
I – the child of starry sky and rolling mist
Initiate of the many mysteries
Foolhardy as I may be
From a dead scripture you continue to read!
While I see what is in the air
And read of the skylines
Ascend & glimpse!

I unravel and shatter
Thy serpentine clasp
Of habituation and attachment
I – of the star-dial'd exile
Forever regaling with beatific delight
For these days are the blessings
We borrow from eternity

Godly Odyssey

My body is the vessel of a godly odyssey
Heaven-bent with passionate abandon
But how was I to know?
That the seeds I was seeking
Were the seeds that no hand has sown

Until then I may bite the brittle bullet;
Brood over its fragile ferocity
But the risks are being run
And I have made a home
Where even the willows couldn't take hold

Slowly, I'll find my place
Between chaos and creation:
Until I discover my true root
Ill never become the tree
That I am meant to be

You may hold open the skies
But keep me from falling through:
Then I will fly only on the cloudflares
And I will take guidance only from the sunsphere
And I will drink only from the soulocean

The alchemy of your embrace
(And fractal expansion therein)
You unmap my tatterdemalion smile
And there is no evidence of expiration,
Yet my eager for the discovery!

I have debouched from the abyss
All about me is the potential for unlimited & endless
My eye shall only find synchronicities as steep as the trees

Casting the fathoms, counting the rain
And a future,
there,
waiting,
for me to catch up!

Against Dystopia

"He crosses a lonesome valley, out of the mythos,
and emerges as if from a dream, seeing that his whole consciousness, the
mythos, has been a dream and no one's dream but his own, a dream he
must now sustain of his own efforts. Then even "he" disappears and only
the dream of himself remains with himself in it."
-Robert M. Pirsig-

I

Dead visuals of the Anthropocene (paints the picture incomplete)
Senses usurping, a self-exilic tendency
Foundations all to erosion-prone
Flat-lining vital signs in vogue
Eminent domain lost to the highway
Barons of any bounty! It's too much
You nothings-off-limits marauders! It's too much

Under these heavy boot heels
My martyred afterlife
Is a death uncounted
From the parsing out
And perforce fractioning
Unyielding imperious, it's too much!
Vainglorious high-flown, it's too much!

Artificial stimuli so life-lacking
As we grow accustom to desert air
With the kindly provided desert view
Tethered by modes of programming
That turns truths into taboo

We've tug to the end of our rope

So push off the moorings!
Are we not always down stream from another!
Paradox-fraught misanthrope, how self-reflective!
Forget not the mirrors in my eyes!

Cycling in the backwash
Of the put-off
Accumulated, sidestepped debt
Sirens wailing at the bloodlet!
Actions in sync to the notes of the tempo
Lost generation and a broken dream
Birthrights bereft
Plundering the unborn child
The future that doesn't go away!

Scenes so severed and incomplete!
For a dream, oft' tis quite terrifying
May we leave more than a legacy of bare dirt and dust?
Perhaps to bestow the early stages of old-growth
May we cycle away from the extinction phase?
Freed from the harness that has us strung
As marionettes,
Biorobots;
A manikin for flaunts

At odds with gravity
From these self-severed wings
Beauty is not that which obeys
Nor is it beholden to thy gaze
Such evidence is found in
The corollary of native sight marginalized

Our surroundings have become scrubland
Because it is our direct reflection
Of all that is being asserted

Of our current subversion –
As the obsolescence that fosters apathy
Eradicating artisanal value-added integrity
Thus works of longevity
Become a withering breed

The put-off has found its outlet now!
And channel to revolt through
As from winter, thy spring anew
Scarified, stratified – ample maturation indeed
To tenderly coax forth
What midnight hath broken clean
Where the shadow stretches further
Than the finest form

Slow thy exodus! We're sinking ourselves
When the gardens can be ours and…

II

I refuse the dystopian dialect!
And subtle devolution --
Narrowed, quickened oblivion
Where our affinity for machines
Has us fit in their likeness
Till so fatally akin to mechanistic
We go without a sound
Gently into every goodnight
O' the grumbling din!
O' the grunting obedience!

The sounds being plowed
And pushed up together
Morphing to a uniform knell
The sound of business as usual

Profitable commodity solely sought
Where our monuments are bare dirt,
Broken ground and the dust kicked up
By the war that tours unremitting

I refuse to march days benighted!
Alone in the hollows of my ghost
Forever followed by bones, vultures and dust
In sallow shades, in corridors withdrawn
The rectilinear diecast, delineated pathway
We're drawn out along

I refuse to perfect lying to myself!
And black out the eyes willfully blind
Learning to live with a downward gaze
Days that become an act of rivers holding back
Only for groundswells to rush all the more fast

I refuse the money-crazed myopia!
Volume-driven, yet never to fill
The empty within me
Such vanities enacted to
Uphold the aggrandized self

I refuse the pants pulled up
An inch by the year
Till the mummy wrappings
And mansions like giant caskets
Swallow us up inside

I refuse the chase for safety!
And dead-reckoning request for certainty
Till the last place we can hide from ourselves is the coffin
A head of stone and a grave blanket of insecurities
We may as well get into the coffin

If all we want is security

I refuse the pipe-dream-poison
Lives lead to perpetuate the profiteering
The exorbitant chapels and
Pedophiliac confessionals
Where holiness is measured
In square footage and ceilings vaulted aloft

You will not make this mountain table-topped!
To accommodate for the low ceilings thus placed
Not I! Not this body of abundance,
With all this beauty surrounding
Not these unfettered wingspans, a metamorphosis fast-gaining

Passer gone blindly by!
No more do you even want off your leash!
Pull out the linchpin! Let thine eye unhinge
Take back thy rightful keep!
Stand up and be counted!
Reclaim thy pristine inheritance!

Whatever be your prison:
This is your escape,
jailbreak,
getaway!

Must it be measured?
Excavating in vain, parts all displaced
Reduced to fragments
Leaving only abject disconnection

Must it be pigeonholed into the uniform mold?
Only to stranglehold
And sink every sun

With a violent undertow

Have we not seen enough? How has this gone unnoticed?
The orbic weathering nature subjects all to
The rounding seasons; any edge made concentric
Have you seen straight lines in a flood, after seasons full circle?

III

Lo, science!
The great infallible ideological bastion
For the mythless, literalist, unimaginative, lost modern man
The new religion whose findings go quite unquestioned
Meanwhile we significantly scrutinize any other source
Ideologically possessed by such methods
Bearing all the same markings and mannerisms as religion
Yet masquerading as it's opposite

Whose measures always prove both sides of the argument
The observation effect of the subjective experimenter
The unaccounted for variables
Imprudent, quick routes to virtue

Venturing to erect another Babel-like tower
That supplants the transcendent
Termites tearing at the temple
Taking objects away from their meaning
Left only with valuelessness

Digging for gold while at the same time making a grave
Taxidermists with clever descriptions
Who must stuff something to study it
Such laborious language must be contrived
To describe what's no longer breathing,
No longer alive

So much talk yet I find myself
Waiting for you to say something!
That which is ever ineffable is your essence
Entrusting the souls depth to human-conceived dogma
Is likely misguided; is the ultimate nature of reality
to be found in objectification?

We are lived by myths
Whose transcendent values orient our aim aloft
This phenomenon isn't contingent
Upon our conscious knowing of it
And therefore I say,
Science alone cannot guide us

But time's dial we cannot turn back:
And what new myth could be so comprehensive,
With a wild breath of such vastness
So as to encompass every tribe, and
Speak to the structure of the modern psyche?

What creature could have broad enough wings
To take us to the place of meaning?
What venerable redemption could instantiate
Our suffering with numinous meaning?
What wind could lift our will to self-transcendence
Without denigrating the earthly and imminent?

Am I woeful to the point of folly
For leaving you more questions than answers?
O what a constellation
Of question marks!

And yet it seems
We cannot go back to Eden

But we can be gardeners of a new forest
With nature as our mirror
We shall move onward
Effulgent with future

IV

Until all of life is the bottom line
And underlays any decision to be made
To set the trajectory for the life to be upheld
And carry on ascending flight in perpetuity

Until this is done the lifeless mediums
Of ill-granting foundations
Will continue to render results
That are a reflection of its cold essence
Allowing obsolescence to foster apathy
Our spirits thus barraged
As we hasten to our own demise

Until this false image is brought down
And the middleman done away with
That will always come between
Ourselves and infinity
And perpetuates a ruinous becoming
As we sell short our deserved
Birthright and inheritance

Until we are known as the sovereign source
Of the quality autonomous and inborn
Accepting the perfection
Of our free-flow sentience
We will not take back our rightful keep

Until the loss is felt as our own

Of the least of these
We will serve only our own
Dog-eat-dog primitive savagery

Until all that which lives, breathes,
And sprouts forth of its own accord
Is raised to assume its rightful, high-rising primacy
We'll hasten on to abysmal tomorrows and a quickened oblivion
As we fish for that which was long ago washed ashore
Busily preparing a funeral bed
Buried long before the eternal slumber

Until a bond is consummated
From the least of these
All the way up to the ultimate transcendent principle
From the bottom of the pyramid to the crest
We will come unhinged in the middle
And amoral scientific rationality will permit anything to occur
Divorced from the myths and values
That give us rooted directionality

Until we hinge our definitions
On a consensual Truth
And discern the patterns of our waking dream
Aligned with reality
We will go on lost on the surface
For science does not have the depth
To direct our behavior
To guide our way of being in the world

Let us form an unbroken covenant
With the sanctity of our Self's integrity
And, in so doing,
Let yourself become a blessing

V

A renaissance awakened
The second coming embodied
In a collective many
Returning swans & broken saints

To encompass the synthesis
The yin and ying harmonization
The great forgiving
The kingdoms homeward pilgrimage

A renaissance reverberates
As waves still break
From the ripples sent out
In the decades of psychedelia

Shall we have the pendulum seek its center?
Or continue the polarized flailing
In time-tangled lies
Of the over-civilized mind

The door has been flung open
The window is wide; the love is there
The healing can happen
We have all the hands to fix it!

Tis a golden age dawning!
And there are billions converging
For there are oceans becoming
The best of all worlds we shall thread together

For the kingdoms becoming
Of this earthen reality
A concrescence of

The flowerful multitudes!

For we are nature's experiment
And, in us, evolution awakens,
Grows emboldened,
& makes a choice

One breed of Being
Within the chaos of Becoming
United in the building of a God
That can carry us well beyond

The ecology of the senses
Coalesces in present awareness,
And language ventures to keep pace
With the changing of faces

Meanings assembles itself
In the space between words;
For a new symbol to be born
From a different center

Will a god save us?
Do we of modernity
Need a myth-generating event
To unite us in meaning?

We wait for patterns to emerge;
Nature has needed lovers
Such as us

VI

For we are the ones who must fight
Just to feel something real

Who must wander toward
Where we can never arrive
Who must give what we can never have
And can never keep
Who must take on the impossible task;

Who must laugh at the hilarious paradox
Of divine irony
As if a human being can be told plainly
What's good for him,
As if what's good for one is good for all;

Who must laugh at tragedy
And all its irremediableness
Constituted by this perilous chorus of opposing forces
We need not seek a cure
For the essential tension of existence
That provides life with its striking dynamism;
That gives way to a greater embrace

Who must exist in an unending mystery
For we *are* that mystery
That seeks to discharge its strength
In the making of meaning
In the building of God
By lending a new myth
In the name of self-transcendence

For we are that mystery
That dares to let itself be fathomed
Like a mountainous vastness
Beautifully wrapped in an enigmatic longing
We shall overcome
And steer clear of the deepest despair
That a vacuum of meaning invites

For we are here now
Us builders of a new temple
The ones who must plug our will to create
Into the inflection point of choice
Not to force another formula
But to accommodate that mystery
To honor the artistic unity and
Aesthetic fullness of life itself
To find our inexhaustible depth
Not by continually digging graves
But in the search for beginnings and meanings
To do more than linger between life and death
To do more than spend life in a perpetual flight
From suffering, from solitude, from Self

We shall live in the present
With our potential ever in sight
That we may eventuate our soul's greatness
That we may rise above
The ensuing dystopia of mind and word

O my comrades be heedful!
Of the call of your potential
Subverted by consumerist gratifications,
Of the mythic templates of your self-discovery
Redirected toward a culturally-designated narrative
O how subtle the transformation
Of art into propagandization!
O how those shallow notes cannot accommodate
The sonorous call of authenticity!
No—unhinged consumerism cannot fill the vacuum of meaning
No, it has never filled the empty within me

Yes, we are the ones

Who must take on the impossible task
Of creating an authentic Self
In a system that would rather
Have us be a machine;
Who must speak the dialect of our soul's depth
And not that of dystopia
Who must honor the *logos,*
Through which things are made divine
Under the aspect of eternity;
That which reveals to our Selves
The weave of being &
The soul's sacred dialogue

Yes my friends, let it be fully felt
As it surges and sings through the wide spaces of your heart,
This feeling that oscillates between abundance and restraint
Between despair and triumph
Let it be so very real
Touched by the daylight of your awakening presence
It shall pass, as it rings out with concentric ripples,
And the impressions you're left with
Will tell you of your Self
And you may take it for a war
This process of violent dynamism
And you may take yourself as the greatest fool
This fatally sweet folly
But who you are is thus discovered

No pre-arranged path can soften the blows
Of tragedy, of malevolence, of dust-covered morality
The secret meanings are yours to bestow
Yes my friends it is inevitably so!
What a privilege, the gaps shall be filled in
The picture shall be made complete

The abundance wants out!
It echoes through the dooms of infinite night sky
Through corridors of forest
It speaks of meaning that none other can critique
Of transcendence unsullied by rationalizing mind
Intimating something beyond itself

We must try our hand at living!
As if the horizon's lips had never yet swallowed sun
As if this supreme achievement were not daily done
To create a wide pure space
For the flowing unbestowed superabundance

O and then!
We must live as if this life is the best thing
We have ever been given
As if our toes hang over the edge of the world
As if we could never lose our way

A rapturous affirmation!
An ecstatically experienced mode
Of knowing this very Earth!

To revolt against complacency & numbness:
Let this be our art,
Let our art be our prayer

And our hearts will be the meeting point
Yes—Nature has needed lovers
Such as us

* * *

PART IV

A MOONSTRUCK TIME

The owls have started watching over
The tides of my unrest
While I lay on a bed of knives
Whittling away every edge
Turning, turning, turning
Nights into mornings

Please don't let me be sentenced to reinterpret
The faded memories, the dead gestures, and every ghost-motion
Nor have my eyes sewn open on
And hands held out for
The phantom other that could have been there

For the past is a drowned landscape
Beyond all reproach;
The pages are gone
Wind back the ancient skies
And time still passes fleetly from thy finger;
The dust has settled on us

Yet I'm tangled back into memories
Of a moonstruck time
When my heart was loud
Like lightning and lion's cry
And I didn't heed the sound
(I'm listening now)

O' how I was dauntless in your gauntlets
Of a thousand thorn and thunders roar,
Black chasms gaping and the titanic weight shrugged
When I left your side
Now I would fringe, I would splinter
At the sheer sight of you

For you live atop a thorny tree
And you live your life
Always wet from their creek

But so it goes between lovers
I'll always hear whispers of the tryst
In the far walks
With my night eye
I would keep watch
And we can be as darkly bright
As the moon to the sea
For the owls are not what they seem…

A Pearl Upon the Cloud-Flown Altar

Noctilucent and luminous
In full beam symmetry
Just risen above the trees
Swollen hemorrhaging
Rose-golden nimbus surrounding

So the moon entered my evening
As a rune flung from the faded visionaries
Bestowing seminal song
Doppelgänger of the sun

Concomitant with night
I behold the steady rise,
Feel the icy stabs of the slow reveal
As truth from a shallowed tongue

The sun's double
Bodied forth to mirror for the darkness
Summoning high the waters
As the sun raises
The virescent and arboreal sea

Cresting the nebulous passage
A pearl upon the cloud-flown altar
Threshing floor for my chrysalis to shed
I supplicate to the shimmering excitement
That thy gaze could be one with mine

She is near

She is near
Lighting me with her silver
Rising enchantment under the skin
As high tides upwardly swim

And frail footsteps
Climb the starry archway
A timid gift
Whose visitation is the rarest

From what celestial loft
Hast thou been brought
To confess radiance
Upon my wilderness?

She Is a Rising Moon

She is a rising moon
Treading starry archways
The clouds were hers to vanquish or fly away with
(Such options her luminosity affords)

She is life's meaning made experiential
She is life's essence intensified
She is light made spherical
She is silence made melodic

She is time metamorphosed into water
Moving through endless dimensions
And why am I crying now?
The moon must be full

Full Moon Ache

Got the full moon ache
Shining serpent gaze
Pierces unflinchingly
This won't be the last
Of the bones turned up

The scars tend to itch
By the broken ground
Noctilucence all-permitting
This won't be the last
Of the dust kicked up

Sanded away, rocks by the waves
Calling sharks to the surface
With this thrashing about
And fury in full

Pernicious influence
Of lunacies sweet hurt
Our waterbodies deracination
And arrhythmia monthly

Cloud Convergence

What be the stakes
Of this cloud convergence?
Perchance to kiss

To be in close communion with
Like graceful leaves to caress
Thy rose petal'd flesh

Longing to lose forms
In the undiluted dissolution:
Whatever shall this take?

For the glide-by
To catch flight
In the spindrifts

Innocent, to be in ascent
Surely could be
Of the espousal

I could read the tearshed
Of the cheek-contour
But would it be of her care?

Flower clusters vine and coil
Her ivory clouds enshroud my rocky peak
Even from distance

With but a glide-by glimpse inside
Evanescent glance contacting irises
I'm contained within this kiss

Finding Confluence

What winds will initiate
This passion play?
(Or be it just smoke I chase?)

For the fingers to align
With the bark grooves
Deeply-notched

Delicate in the embrace
Heedful not to rupture
Thy persimmon skin

But to she would I be
Bruised fruit windfallen?
For picking around the purple

Perchance her trickling drops
Weave into my
Threadbare sinews

And finding confluence
We become contiguous
Bloodlines to merge and twine

My gates I hold open
Enrapt for the rivers continuum
To feel this flood pulse union

Of the quickening currents
Wavelengths white-breaking
Tumified consummate for this kiss

Ephemeral Fragility

I woke to the wonder of her
Coming out in a cloudwash
Wandering upon moonbeams
Spread in a spectrum of painted electric

Like a true maiden
So too she foregoes
The slow shade –
Straight to the astral scenery

Yet she tore past gently sudden
With one claw in heaven,
With ephemeral fragility

Giving any the impetus to move
Firekeeper! You hold the stars
Budding within your vestal eye
Around which I must constellate

Here I am batting lashes about
As I try to untie the flame lengths
With moth wings

Taken up by the mandate of your love
I'm like an autumnal leaf at winter's approach
Flamed to red then falling into orbit

Melted away by movements like liquid crystals
Tis a price beyond all pearls
To have a swan visit your shore

Your Heart is a Vast Land

Your heart is a vast land
And I am a mapmaker

Your veins are aching waterways
And I am a riverkeeper

Your freckles form wondrous constellations
And I am an astronomer

Your lips are fragile as rose petals
And I am a gardener

I can't explain it
But your eyes compel me to try
They hint to the mystery of why
The horizon was never wide enough for your lovely smile

And that I may be the only mariner
Fit for the voyage into your oceanic eyes
To see the dream that hides inside
(And the sun that's still to rise)

I can feel this
Within the compass of my bones
Where the marrow moves
For your lunar force

O' My Freelance Orbit

O' my freelance orbit!
That makes full swing
Of the concentric rippling
A butterfly balletic!
A feathered touch!
How indelible be the door which
Leads me to her lips
(The eye of my swirling pursuit)
And summons inception
Of a resonant reaction
Expression for expression
Perfectly reflected
Rhythmic proportions accordant
As intonations of morning
The stately grace
And winsome youth
That allures with
The shadows cast
From her comely curves
Blending through borders
Loosening limbs
I espy well past
Where ripples end
To the vista
Ill always remember
Yet never does it end
With a soft opening
As flowers to the spring
It soars toward the source
By bolt or bloom
Always going to seed

As Flowers Flow

As flowers flow
From the virginal green
So to you does
My love spring

As flaming arrows fly
Midst the star-dial'd alignments
So to you these dreams burn
Which no cloud could eclipse

As waves dash and leap
From an immaculate breeze
So too does my rhythm dance for you
With quickening heartbeats

As a field is fashioned in flames
By the bolts of midsummer's heat
So too am I thunderstruck
When consummately our eyes meet

And I'm in Love Again

...And I'm in love again
With the sky that has never been
And will never be again
Each and every sight,
A flower to my eye
Each and every sound,
A song to crown the silence
Lost in the intertwining melodies
Of You – Of Us

And I'm in love again
With the wind in the trees
Playing a song I have never heard
And the flowers leaping
From the fertile earth,
With this sense of infinity and magic implied
By the elements of Earth expressed as Beauty
As I find Your Name
Upon my breath

* * *

Part V

When a Poet Falls in Love

Heaven help us, for
When a poet falls in love
Nothing is safe from his poetic decadence
With every breath he will erect a new temple
That it may be worthy of her gaze,
If only to be sanctified by her eyes

With every syllable he will spin great fables
All too forgetful of the ephemeral
As if it won't be gone by dawn,
As if the cosmic impossibility of their meeting
Is an occasion for parables,
As if his every yesterday need be christened by a new mythology

Thusly his mind will go on composing grandiose oratory
Such as *seeing Her was like the first time I heard silence,*
And these many such discursive interjections
Will seek some symbol to catch the projections
As if reality itself hadn't just redeemed him
With an undeniable, irrevocable proof

As if reality hadn't furnished
The perfect dream-shape to fit into
The correspondingly proportionate emptiness within,
He takes to words again and again
To leave no meaning unspent
Himself being so prone to squander

Ah, let him drown a thousand hopeless ships! He may learn
To sail after all; he may discover a new & secret flower
And learn what the gardeners have always known:
That beauty is akin to death
And he must get better at dying

If he is to survive the fury of Her beauty

Who else if not him will make dramatic and loquacious verses
About the flowers and the wind,
And all those thousandfold never-ending things
That remind him of the Beloved, of the Friend?
Who else if not Her will help him understand how the lover
Becomes the Beloved?

And while it may be true that to a poet
Everything looks like a flower,
Could mere words be a fitting tribute
To the vertiginous altitudes
She would take his heart to?
Lets just hope that he learns the charm of brevity soon…

What if these passing statues could never
measure up to a proper homage?
And why on earth would this fool want to remind himself
Of that divine madness called Love? O that sacred daze of
Recklessly blooming incomprehensible fullness
Ah, for the aliveness it did provide!
(As if he found death's antidote)

Perhaps a few saccharine verses, verging on the idolatrous,
Will help him make sense of his mind's tumult
And, if nothing else, be a way to shake his fist
At the vagaries of impermanence—
Ah, let him enjoy the aesthetics of his foolishness
With royal amusement!

Perhaps his curiously extravagant proclamations
Will strike a euphonious note and tempt providence
Or maybe, within him,

Today's sky will ripen
To the point of song
When the poet falls in love

Today's sky will ripen
To the point of song
When the poet falls in love

When I Go Looking for Flowers

Where to go?
When you can say I love you anywhere
And call the butterflies
To complete the invocation
For love comes in a moment
To bridge the distance

But are you the one
Of whom I'm told I will find
When I go looking for flowers?
Or the one who will arrive
When I call the butterflies?

Don't just say it is
If that's not what you meant
'Cause I would hold open the sky
If only for your light

I Saw Shining

I saw shining,
Skin lit holy;
Breast of your awakened flesh
A goldrush of vagrant light rays
Spiraling into your starseed eyes
Laying bare thy beauty marks

Interlacing mosaics of cloud,
Infusions of wonder give chase
Are you my transient messenger?
My prophet of this moment?
Seeding the sundream,
Spreading fistfuls of dawn

Unwearied, I'm free for a moment
From the habitual repetitions
Unfettered, my wing-spans fast gaining
And I am risen to witness the sun-kissed splendor of her
O the geometric perfection, so effortlessly majestic,
I'm left breathless…

I caught suddenly the shining meaning
Of sunbeams breaking,
Weightlessly, against your being
And then you came to me
Like the sun comes
To the sleeping

I Will Never Understand

I will never understand
How you could hold together
The whole wild sky with those
Small yet royal branches
Which form your hands

No, it's not at all clear to me
How this is achieved:
How you keep straight
The vanishing expanses & many-hued arrays,
Gently mixing in some watercolor-clouds

And how do you manage to collect
Water from every ocean
And cast it across azure distance
To curate such musical storms?
(Which you so graciously showcase for spring)

Pray tell me how you rise, of a morning,
Endure the radiant tones of your firesong,
And build a world with light
—A world where all songs are possible
(Where everything [even God] is possible;
Where even we can meet)

And then there's that space in the midst of your arms,
That loudly flowering meadow was a place
Where swarms of disorientation couldn't quite find me
Ornamented as it was with its
Decorous echoes & flights of silence
The major and minor notes blended with such subtleness
(How heedlessly you surround me with gardens
When you tell me who you really are)

Therefore you might understand
How I would be so prone to calling it home—
If it weren't so adorned with transitoriness,
If it weren't for those elegiac farewells
So destined yet so intolerable

Ah—but don't let this suggest that I seek forgetfulness
For now that's a luxury I can do without;
How could it be any other way?
Meaning assembles itself between us, ineffably,
In these ways I still attempt to understand

A Lover's Soul

What do lovers really seek: separation or union?

Who can bear the peril
Of being cast out into the fathomless ocean
Of a lover's soul?

And yet, I went toward her
With that kind of fervor
That a river has as it carves vast valleys to reach the sea

Who can fare the fragility
Of flowers opening to spring?
O that blossoming velocity!

And yet, I found my wings when it was time
To fly to the other side of tomorrow
Where seeds in their season could reveal light

How does one stay with the intensity
Of feeling into Her infinite effulgence?
O that blissful oblivion!

To be as the meadow at the top of the world
Where the mountain wind let's loose
Her unbound melody

How does one stay casual in the midst of it all?
Upon noticing that I am forever in The Presence
I try not to make a scene

But it makes we want to throw everything else away
And spend up all of my love
On offerings to The One

How does the grandeur of God
Stay contained beneath this flesh?
Like the pool that receives the waterfall's impact

How does one always follow
The flow of the soul's echo?
O how I hark to those waves unrelenting

And venture to move Heaven & Earth
That I may track the watercourse way
Of a lover's soul

THE SEASONS OF HER HEART
(BRIDE OF THE WIND)

"Even your absence is filled with your warmth
And is more real than your not-existing"
-Rainer Maria Rilke-

I

We were the Lovers
Who lived within the garden walls
Drinking from each other's irises the deathless nectar,
Building whole languages from the meanings implied
By the slightest gaze—from that unabashed,
Sacrosanct domain—where the violent winds
Are unable to lay waste
The winter's citrus blossoms

But,
The seasons of her heart can change in an instant:
Spring can jump to Fall and back to Summer again
Before your eyes have time to blink
So Friends, there's no reason fighting it,
Some things are as they will always be;
The space between two mirrors
Is pure

Yet
Subject to mercurial winds:
It shall carry on this way until the water runs clear,
Until the feeling is fully felt, nevertheless
You will be trying to make an atlas
To chart the prodigious vastness of her many moods
As if you're some kind of clever astronomer
Studying the phases of the moon

So,
You'll have to excuse me, if I'm
Reaching for meaning on empty wintry branches
But, having once played a part in the sacred seasons of her heart,
Indulge me and heed these words:
Every garden is a gamble—
So often God has other things in mind,
Doesn't he?

II

Anyway Friends,
There's no reason fighting it:
Just let her level you with her eyes, (*anyway*)
Let her cast the arrows of her gaze
Far into your heart
(*Anyway*)

Let her unravel your knotted depths
And outwit your defenses, (*anyway*)
It may be your undoing, but let her teach you
More about yourself than you even really knew
And be your impetuous revelation
(*Anyway*)

Let her bring this swirling world to a standstill
And turn sand back into stone, (*anyway*)
Let her lure you from your brooding
And be the medicine for your world-wearied soul, (*anyway*)
Let her great radiance draw you into this world
And make the whole game worth playing
(*Anyway*)

Let her beauty be a prophecy of that

Which you may come to know within yourself, *(anyway)*
And then let her go back to the otherside of tomorrow
Back to her hallowed isle
Back to her home in the mouth of a flower
(Anyway)

Let her go again so she can be
The bride of the wind that she is, *(anyway)*
That songstress who surpasses the roses
With the bloom of her song
(Anyway)

Let her, even though you'd do anything to make her stay
Even though you'd bear any other weight
Cause no weight could be so great
As the weight of her absence
(Anyway)

Let her,
And this whole dizzying dance,
Lead you back into the gardens
Which you exiled yourself from
(Anyway)

Because honestly, it is worth enduring
The winds & serpents that hide in every paradise, *(anyway)*
And what passing cloud could eclipse your heart's devotion?
(Though it only serves to illustrate your naïveté)
(Anyway)

Because honestly,
God wouldn't have it
Any(other)way

Days of Roses & Embers

"The Eternal Feminine lures us to perfection."
-Goethe's Faust-

I

I'm dancing in the garden
Of your melodies
I'm fasting on the light
Of your love
And it's more than enough
To get me by
O I'm nearly drown
In this oceanic feeling!

Your eye shines with a spark of the divine
That opens the seed within my soul
I'm quenched by your kisses
Cause they kiss me from within
And my heart, at last, feels whole
As if we made a bond before we were born
Before we took on this fleeting form
Now the infinite is imminent with you

I feel like I finally found you
And the years leading me here
Were just to prepare for this
Yearned for union
As if I was a young river traveling seaward
For an ocean that would not refuse my flow
Waiting my whole life to find;
The ceaseless searching

But is one lifetime enough

To behold all of your lush landscapes?
(O' your wonders beyond all words!)
Or to fathom the full depth
Of your immense and boundless beauty?
(O' its more than I've ever been told!
More than any sum of gold)

Well, I shall make this one enough
Cause I want to see
Every hidden vista
Of your scenic world
So I'll be like the migrant bird
Flying to your seasons heat
Like the butterfly drawn to the call
Of the love-bloom within you

O my lady of the eternal spring
Within your eye I find Eden enduring

II

Since last we embraced
And I was swept up
In the floodtides of your touch
In the winds of your rosewater-scent
A trembling leaf in your sweet breezes
Amidst the wondrous constellations
Of your freckles and impeccable skin
(Every part of you shines like a flower to my eye)

I have traced back the tracks,
The prints of your every kiss
And how I count them like blessings
My skin yearns for them again
As a desert yearns for rain

And counts every drop that has fallen
(My Love, you must be from the mouth of a flower)

I gather warmth from
The fire of our union
For now its appears to be carried on
By the embers of memory
Yet my yearning burns
With unfading adoration
(Onward I gladly travel past the limits of my longing)

I had nine days to breathe you in,
Nine nights to crystallize *us*
Amidst the swoons and ripened silence
And I found the mirror in your eyes
You are the melody to my rhyme

I can't even believe it
How the time ran wild
And those hours turned into days
I shall always hold those moments
As precious treasures

Now, here I am between two mountains
And you have flown over oceans
It feels like my river can't reach the sea
Until the flood comes once more
And we are again unified in physicality

Your love has gotten into my blood
Ever since our souls touched
And my heart is humming like a tree full of bees
The garden of my senses has grown wild with vines
Each tendril spiraling to embrace you
Forever-enamored by your singing smile,

By your full-moon-eyes that never seem to wane

I dream of the day
When you will again
Take me into your arms
Pulling me closely to your chest
And I will listen with bated breath
To your sweet heart-rhythms
And there in that ecstatic stillness…

I will gift to you all that I am
By way of a kiss
Unto your fragile, rose-petal lips
(Like a flower bends towards the sun with all its love)

You deserve the devotion of a man's heart:
One who will sing your divine glories
Like the birdsong that heralds the dawn
(And I want to tell it from a mountaintop)

One who will forever plant poetry
Within the garden of your heart
And be a perpetual spring of inspiration to you

One who will ground you yet give you flight
Holding the space for your truth
Never eclipsing your inner light

One who will let you dance freely
In the truth of who you are
Allowing you to be the original authentic expression
Of your sacred design

One who will never become complacent or ungrateful
With the gift of your heavenly presence

Never forgetting that you are like the spring
That brings the leaves back to the trees

One who you can trust and know
Will stay as sturdy as the Oaks
Yet retaining the flexibility
To bend with the stormwinds of change

One who will love every part of you
Even the parts you may frown upon,
I will kiss them with impassioned abandon!
That your soul's beauty may be known

O' you have dawned so many dreams in me
Together we can do anything
We help each other become
What we are made to be
And I want to take part
In this sacred art
Of being better together
Of growing in love
As
One

III

She would count the rain
As I would count the fallen leaves
For I was of the forest
And she was of the seas

But what am I to thee,

A waif in your white breakers?
And what are you to me,

The lightning that scars bark,
That splinters?

IV

I don't think I'll ever be the same
Now that I know your name
Now that I've seen your face

Surely these seeds were sown so long ago
And though we know the leaves change
When comes the autumn,
My love for you, no season can sway
Summer-colored it will always stay

In your still waters I find my reflection
Your smile brings down pieces of heaven
I may not own many things
But with you I am rich
Beyond any worldly wealth

My love for you: does it go without end?
It must, for I've yet to see
Sign of a horizon

V

In these months I have loved you
With many lifetimes worth of fervor
There is something marvelously familiar
About your carob tint of your skin, about your cheeky smile
That makes it easy to give all that I am for this Love of Ours

Perhaps it was our imperfections that brought us together
That made us perfect for each other

O' my wildflower, I will endure the thorns!
Despite all the fragile and ephemeral things that elude my grasp,
Your beauty is not lost on me

The sun inside of me wants nothing more than to give you warmth
I have lost track of where your sea begins and my sky ends
I drink deep of you, entwined in a union divine
I keep falling further and further in love with you
So let us go where there is no road

We shall make a shrine of the sun, moon and stars
They will be our royal company
And there will be nothing left to chance
Any answer we ask for, the sea will write it in the sand
And there we will find God's guidance

Threading us through the heart of the stars
To find the sweetest shelter, the home here in your arms
Cause our love lives where no dust gathers
And all the hours of forever will never find us
Within our whimsical world

VI

The prophecy of our love
Was written in the flicker
Of constellations,

Mentioned in the whispers
Of mutual friends,
And fulfilled by our synchronistic whims

God has shown me so many things
And yet, you are more
Than all the gardens I've ever seen

O' how I have prayed
That your wandering footsteps
Would lead to me

Maybe it was your sweet song I heard
Echoing across all those miles of blue
That led me to you

If I am given just these transient moments
To spend with you
I will still regard it as a gift

For you are the blessing
That I am always counting
And I don't know how to love you any less

"Is it my redemption or my ruin?"
The question that beckons all lovers
To wonder of this terrifying & beautiful fate called Love

What ever be the verdict I will gladly endure it
For pain is a small price to pay
To feel such a real thing as Love

VII

A flower that has thorns
Urges us to handle it
All the more gently

A tender blossom wants to know:
That her petals are safe to unfold,
That she can open her heart
As wide as the sky

Without fear of any harm

So the Sun holds her lightly
But just tight enough
That she may lift her wings
And send the dream of a seed
To reach for those golden echoes
That lie on the other side of tomorrow

VIII

Have I told you lately
Just how beautiful you are?
What words could I possibly conjure
To make you understand my adoration?

Shall I summon the wind?

As for me? Well I'm just the same as I ever was:
Your currents still carry me
Down waterfalls into the sea
Like I'm driftwood in some windswept dream

Did you summon the wind?

Have I told you lately
Just how much I love
The shape of your body
Outlined by sunlight

Shall I summon the wind?

When we reached out to fetch the furthest star
We plucked petals of the sun
Our makeshift wings were bound to burn

But your scorching skies, I have not forgot

Did you summon the wind?

IX

I'm with you when distance leaves nothing near
I'm here, always here

And for a moment
I forgot my fears
And dared to love you
With abandon, without the need
Of a promise
Unfettered by expectation

That's when I learned of
The power that comes
When your love
Is freely given; O I swear I'll be
Content with the glimpses and visions
That come in the season they're given

I can feel you slipping away
Like a dream in the morning
Just after waking up
Like lines of poetry
That flee too quickly
Back to eternity

I can feel you coming back to me
Like a dream in the midnight
That I don't want to wake from
So sleep on it even if I may be
Awake in your dreaming

Steep me in the leaves of your dreams

Even if I'm sleepless as the moon
And restless as the sea

X

Haven't I done my dying?
In the golden fires of her horizon
O how many ships I sunk to the song of that siren
O how many ships I jumped
To be there beside her
(O bind me to the ships mast,
stuff my ears full of wax!)

Haven't I done my dying?
And for too long now
Lived life like I'm in exile
Looking outside for the mirror in your eyes
To keep me from going blind
But you showed me that
To look within is to awaken

Haven't I done my dying?
And O how I would do it all again and again
If I were reissued that time, on you I would spend it
For the arc of my days has been Heaven-bent ever since
How my spirit quickens at the mention of her name
Must I wait until the next life?
Is it a fool's errand to wait?

XI

The moonlight was a silver whisper
Darkly bright like the strands of your hair

That I keep finding everywhere

As onward we wander
Toward the restless beckoning of destiny
But when am I going to see you again?

Was it that I walked right into
Your life at the wrong time?
Or you into mine?

Even still
Just knowing you
Makes me a better man

"Ephemeral", said the wind to the sky
One feather at a time
But what am I to thee?

O how we always did
Know each other from the inside
I never had to guess

So why is it I am listening
For these silver whispers
In the forest darkness?

As silence now spreads
Its heavy wings
Between us

XII

O lovely One,
You whom my heart once chose
Was that your ghost I saw upon

The trails and vistas
That I rove?

O lovely One,
Do you still recall
When we became love,
In that meadow made of gold,
And how the oaks did behold?

And those wild strawberries scattered around?
How, for those uncounted moments,
Nothing else existed?
And I beheld your gorgeous face
Gently rapt in the sun's warm embrace

O lovely One
Forgive my folly—
Did I see that day clearly?
Or was I wrapped in fog?
Such loveliness I had never known
And you gave me blue skies
When you told me nothings wrong

O lovely One
O what a dream we live
O what beautiful moments
We got to spend
Laughing our way into consummation

Unwrapping as two the one eternal present
Of our soul's own effulgence
Thus to discover the rapturous, luminous truth
Of love revealing itself:
To us, through us
Of us, because us

As us, for us
With such
Tender
Innocence

O that innermost experience of ultimate togetherness!
O how it made me forget my every idea of paradise
For that dream to have wakened in the midst of reality
Was my closest notion of utopia—
That feeling I will remember forever

XIII

How was I to know that
This love was inside of me,
Had it not been for you
Whose presence called it forth?

Like a fortuitous wind upon sleeping embers,
Like a seed so suddenly
Surrounded by springtime—
That's what you were to me

And now I look out across the water,
I can't help but thinking
That I'm going to see you there
(Such are the secrets I keep with the sea)

But still I want to have flowers prepared
(As would the spring)
For we part only to meet again
In another song, in another garden

* * *

PART VI

Unopened Scrolls

"There is only one thing I dread: not to be worthy of my sufferings."
-Fyodor Dostoevsky-

There's an ancient book within you:
Unopened scrolls of living scripture
A temple filled with sacred texts
That only your eyes can read,
That only you can enter

It lies in wait:
Until we travel to the extent of our pain
And go into that dungeon of denied feelings,
That storm that seldom rests,
Thus to actually find that your hidden nature
Is really a gorgeous wilderness

Your soul is
Like an old poem
That slowly reveals itself
And you don't know till it's happening,
Then, all at once, it's breathing you—
It is He who wants to know Himself as You;
It is He who wants You to meet your Self

So go forth, toward the within
As even now, the moment already dissolves
Yet the hour is ever yours:
Part those tempestuous waters
To wander inside the swollen ocean

If you still see the flickering and fading
Waves upon the surface,
You've not gone far enough

If you see those unutterable extents,
Beset on all sides, then you are well nigh

Thunder will come when it does,
But your emancipation is inevitable;
The chrysalis cracked long ago
Cast off the last mummy wrappings
And discover all those unopened letters
That God has been sending your heart—
Who else could possibly do it for you?

Your soul is
That one love poem
God keeps writing to himself
Just to have reflected his beauteous essence

Hidden Wings

You hide your wings so well
Prostrate under the weight
Of the world

And how often it feels as though
Not even the ground
Would receive your shadow

Even if every attempt to lift
Has you back in the ashes
Still it is better than staying buried away

Because you are more
Than what your wounds
Make you do

And all the ways you still flinch
And react to past afflictions hence
Know you have never been lovelier
Than as you are now

But as you confront
The gulf between who you are
And who you are to be
Gently consider:

That your greatest blessing
Is your deepest wound
And the descent that it precipitated
Was the impetus your wings needed to grow;
They were forced to fledge in that free-fall

Traversing your perilous depth,

You're given the conditions which your wound
Manifested for it's own healing—
The same path by which your gift is rendered
Thus, the wound becomes a womb
From whence you're born unto your boon

That's the ferocity of Grace forcing your hand
By giving you the upper hand
Of being sent all the way down
To taste the hellish ashes; and
It's the very taste of those cinders
That makes you remember
Your hidden wings

O' Temporal Apparition

"Time glides in secret and his wings deceive;
nothing is swifter than the years."
-Ovid, *Metamorphoses, Book X*-

O' temporal apparition
Don't you know?
Eternity has nothing to do
With time

And all this talk of God
Don't you know by now?
It surely does not prove
Your grasp of Truth

You've probably just
Looked into (or avoided)
Too many mirrors lately
And thus deluded & diluted your vision

It's really a lot to expect,
As if you can just pull on
One thread of the spider's web
And avail yourself of all meanings

Now you must shake off
The jet lag of landing in this body
And the baggage of past lives
Even if this suit of skin often fits too tight

And when you feel
All too trapped within this flesh
Thoroughly dizzied by
The spiral of reflections

Remember how this grandiose dilemma
Could easily be seen as lamentable,
But by now you should surely know?
These seeds were sown so long ago

O' temporal apparition
You don't have to always be the hero;
Not matter how much magic you find inside
You still got to take your time

A Wind without Origin

I go everywhere collecting keys
That unlock the knots
Made by when the spirals of my thought
Melodically meander upon each other

Along the way, the scenes I see
I'm unsure if I have or have not
Seen them in another dream
—It doesn't have to make sense
But such is the fragility of perception

Is there truth to be found
In that which is imagined?
I sill wonder which is more real:
The object or its reflection?
Is it that we use objects, or they use us?

I still wonder why
Everything is changing all around us
But I meet so many others
And we already know each other
From the inside

Admittedly, I've been a man of extremes:
On days when I feel alive
I call out across the waves to the horizon
As if I will live forever
And at the most faint sign of rain
I have been known to get the notion
To plant a flower garden

There are also those days
Where I feel like a lonesome mountain lion

Going years without ever really being seen
On cliffs exposed, where the eagles are flying low
And not for anything other than Love
Would I let myself be glimpsed
By different eyes than the sky's

But I really do need
A garden I can get lost in
With the most precocious flowers,
And a poem I can nearly drown in
Finding each word as a sunken treasure

Maybe it's a fool's pursuit
Maybe the lottery has already been won
Maybe I long ago excavated the hidden crown
Maybe love itself is the pain of being truly alive
Maybe the rain is truly innocent

Just the same—
My name needs enough space to forget itself
So that, whatever latitudes I'm called to,
I'll always arrive on time
Cause I'm from everywhere, like the sky
And at the same instant
A wind without origin
What locks or keys could ever keep me
From ending up at the entrance?

Quite a Meeting

Sons and daughters
Of the great kings and queens of old
You who make a bed of the mountains
You who find ineffable meaning
In the blue of the ocean
You who draw life's flame from sun through blood

This life is quite worth
The presence of your prayers
Forego the temptations
To split thy attention
On that which is inconsequential

You who circle round
The revolving door of the seasons
You who stood up in an infinity of unlikeliness
You who availed yourself within this ghost of a chance
You who find yourself always gazing
Deep in the sky where no clouds dare wander

Search to find that which will make you lost;
Leave some space for things to come undone
Lest you imprison all potential
Seek not perfection;
But ask for the ability to *see* it

You who have been knocking at the door
Until flesh permitted entrance
Who kept knocking
Until the separation was made complete
So a union could be possible
You who have been unknowingly mourning Adam's fall

Let your eye find paradise
In the most common sight
Ecstatic wonder is thy birthright
Gather strength by giving thanks
And be guileless of the consequence

You who also hollowed out a home
In these carbon bones
I've never met you
And you've never met me
But when we see each other again
I know it will be quite a meeting

WHAT DOES IT MEAN TO SEE?

What does it mean to see?
—The question that reckons

From the watchtower atop
The scaffolding of my bones
The patterns of smoke; maps of my mind
Forged through the topographical scatter of echoes
Something melodious is strung together
But one leaf alone makes no sound

What should be made irrelevant?
—Is the better question

Relevance determines perceived reality
Often my world consists of
The space of a single letter
Or it might coalesce with
A single emerald needle
Suspended midair by gossamer

Does immediacy predict
What we can forget?

You might be amazed
Of the pathways that surface
If you don't look away
If you stop letting your sight
Skip across the surface of space
Not quite sinking in, unarrived

So value determines
The content of vision?

Portals of perception open and close, fleetingly
Then you're back in between meanings
With the concomitant chaos
Another desert to be wandered
Back to drawing water from the stone
The bottled connotations

Grabbing hold the reins of the eyes
I'll probably spend my whole life learning to see

What To Do?

I

There's so much in this world that's not
Right here

Contemplating my place in eternity
I feel terribly tiny

There's so much I want to do that would require me
To be the size of an ant

There's so much I want to do that would require me
To be the size of a planet

What to do?

I drift back and forth between these feelings
Of grandiosity and worthlessness

Were we once of the same
Constellation?

Were we once of the same
Heap of dust?

There's so little I know; I prefer what I don't
I think I'll leave the sword in the stone

Tell me your theories; I want to hear
The choirs of your mind

Because I fall prey to thinking
In absolutes

My being lacks nothing
And still I long for You

(A kind of longing that makes you wonder
if you can live a minute longer)

What to do?

II

What is this impenetrable distance
Between the world and myself?

As if I'm some far planet doomed only to orbit
And never quite enter & apprehend

Some kind of sound that forgot
How to echo back

Some kind of ripple that forgot
How to find shore

As though the world backs away at my advance,
Or am I the one pushing back?

One leaf alone makes no sound
Or am I too far away to hear it yet?

Maybe I'm just planting the seeds
Too deep in the ground

III

You call me to great distances, infinitely far

My life barely feels big enough to encompass

I must be the seed sown by the wind
With haphazard precision

Even as I build You
I know it will never be finished

I learn most about You
When I have experiences of love

Or is it when I reach injunctions
Of suffering that I learn most?

—It must be when I admit
How truly human I am

Like gathering drops of dew
I've only known glimmers of You

We yearn to launch ourselves into eternity
Through the window of this moment

I birth my eternity
With a sense of indebtedness

I'm like a beggar
Who wouldn't squander so much as a crumb

We see what's happening
Through such a small screen

I try to be satisfied
With just a thumbnail sketch

But I always seem to be
Peeking through the keyhole

With a jeweler's scope
To get more than a glimpse

Of the architect's master plan
And the discernable patterns therein

The conception of God as *only* light
Can be a very problematic connotation

At best it is one way to invite
A terrible confusion into the mind

For we are always stumbling in a deep darkness
And I for one feel compelled to rejoice

(Maybe it's because I know every backroad
From here to Hell)

There's a space around me that grows vast
And I don't want to take in any other voices

Still I will speak You
As if no one has ever tried before to call forth your riches

THE SILENCE OF A WILD PLACE
-An ode to Sonoma County-

That the silence of a wild place
Makes the air more pure there
She suggested to me
And she was aglow with a deep meaning
And twilight shone upon those hills a golden shade of dreams
—O' the sanctitude that resounded therein

It was a temple if there ever was one:
An overlook of some secret valley
Where moments of reverence find *you*——
You need not seek to find *them*
You don't even need to close your eyes
To feel the humming hive inside

That's the kaleidoscopic possibility of the present
To mount the hugeness of the moment as that of a mountain range
Most things are unsayable, *I reluctantly admit*
But maybe language is that which liberates
And nothing is too small to be unnamed
We just never have anything more than a moment to do it justice
And that's alright with me right now

Are we wrong to be seeking symmetry in such tangled places?
I seem to have a fondness of chaotic perfection
Of the sort that wants to become words,
That wants to be loved like its already gone
—Because it's already gotten into the wind
And that's alright with me now

Is it the unforgettableness of a place
That hallows it so? That makes it exalt these moments?
Such a question suggests its own answer

But do go on and gently destroy me with your beautiful words
Tell me of those things you only say to your heart
I have ears for the unheard

The Thought of Her

She said,
To let the nights come and go
As through an open window,
And let these days
Tremble in the wake of our becoming

Said he,
Blessed be that mystery which allows us to participate
In our own divinity, which allows us to partake
In courtship of opposites; to share meaning & discover
More of one's Self through the eyes of the Other

And her beauty held him spellbound, as if it were
Immaculately gathered from some secret place
And he remembered the weight of all that might come
—His eyes scarcely glimpsing
The marionette strings of fate

Yet he also felt this winged vigor
That changed weight into wind;
That made its way into his innermost feeling
Across all the lighted miles of inner distance
And scarcely was he aware of this nearness,

Of this indistinguishable taking and giving, and
The highly dynamic tension that gives way to a greater embrace
Never had he longed like this:
Miles of time tried to pry the remembrance from his mind
But each day its force returned anew

He had not yet encountered
Something so undyingly persistently
As the thought of Her; many means he did seek

For his mind to truly stray
But it engulfed the widest horizon of the brightest sky

Not even the arms of another lover
Could extinguish the remnant embers
Of the thought of Her;
Not yet had he encountered
Something so veritably unbearable

And he would watch
As words blurred to resemble her name
And he would listen
As sounds would evoke the melody of her voice
And this both haunted and bewildered him

But the trees still knew his name
When they quivered with spontaneous wind
And from this he gathered calm again
Because it looked like freedom
Because its sound reminded him of life

THIS STRANGE NOSTALGIA

What is this strange nostalgia
For something that never was?
The future must be growing inside me;
Drifting into remembrance of potentials & painted visions
The past breathes with new meaning
As it's vanishing at the crossroads of here & now:
It'll have to do

What wants to become segues seamlessly
—If you follow your *yes*
But why am I enamored with what vanishes?
Is it that things are more fleeting to increase their potency?
I must be suspended in the tension between reverie and reason
Let us linger in the twilight anyway:
It'll have to do

Follow Beauty
-An ode to Big Sur-

I follow beauty like I'm searching
For the attributes of my lost divinity
Inexhaustibly, my soul shall quest for its grace
Mysteriously led to mythic & pristine places:
Of cloud-hidden ridgelines & verdant sea meadows
I'm stoned on stars at the edge of my perception

Under the canvas of a cloud-brushed sky
I take flight somewhere within myself
Not to flee from this moment, though,
But to see the world in lovely & becoming colors
And recover my lost myths

The freedom I'm looking for
Involves retrieving pieces of myself
That were lost to the infinite
Like hunting for jade after winter storms
Along the intertidal lines

Seeing is my church
And these things need infused by your viewing
Because one doesn't just *see* an ocean:
Your senses lift in unison like a murmuration of seabirds
Thus to commune with your soul

Breathe with me as
Utter profundity drives me to silence
Breathe with me while
Drinking from waterfalls
Breath with me before
Time catches up with us

Breath with me and
Spontaneously meet the moment
By following beauty
Let us toil for the fulfillment
Of the patterns we've been given
By following beauty

Sonnet to the Plum Blossom

A new spring has found its way back to the trees
And finally! something in which I can believe:
O the plum blossoms softly opening by imperceptible degrees
With impossibly delicate gestures—

An inward dimension they seem to open from
And though I am not quite so delicate as they,
Perhaps I too am innocently beholden to an ancient cycle
And something of me purposefully endures through winters

Perhaps I too am fertile with future
And, in a desire to express the many-colored melody
Of this tremendous inwardness, have sought to invent flowers

Perhaps I too feel the texture of my breath
Similarly to the way they paint with pollen a dark meadow
Perhaps I too am finally beginning

Mystery of the Rose

It's in the breathing mystery of the rose,
Exhibiting in plain crimson an exulted quality,
Whose gestures express an enchantment,
That my eye accommodates itself unhurriedly
To a purity inviolate of misinterpretation
Wherein one forgets about what is lofty

You whose being breaks past
The field of my meanings
Thy rapture does not confer imposing notions
But rather makes wonder anew and unconcealed

And I find this weightlessness
To be positively vertiginous
Where the sense of mystery communicates itself
There are no horizons

And that's not even what's worth noting:
What's worth noting is that
Fragile yet hopeful countenance
That bespeaks a knowing which lives within mystery
Yet abides invisibly with guileless surprise
The secret rapture, which composes notes
Of meaning from being, of sense from spirit

That interior space of undiminished grandeur
Between the folds of the rose
Where mystery itself comes to rest

Rather Than Arriving

"All that is transitory is but a metaphor."
-Goethe-

Rather than arriving, a flower is
Constantly exploring its own open-endedness
The petals appear to be sails cast open
Preoccupied with a spontaneous vision
In a wordless way I hear voices upraised to the point of song
And heedfully the bees come to be stung with a fine intoxication
These productions from nothingness are constructions
In which time can rhythmically exist,
Are allegorical of themself, are symbolic if nothing else—

Ah, but what is this urge to statically arrest
The image into symbol, into history?
To turn away from the living edge of petals,
The innumerate folds & voluptuous weave of subdued intensities,
And place the gaze at a retrograde angle
Toward the ghosts & eidolons in tow

Look, I'm trying not to call attention to the frailty
And constantly possible collapse of the exaggerated subtlety
These are grounds for a familiar notion: of infinite destinations
That carry their connotations of time, but
The mind can only make so many circles before it wavers, again,
At the spontaneous form, and therefore

Rather than arriving, *our* every gesture
Is provisionally given to the next instant
With an eye to what the next wave will become
Harmoniously integrating what is with what is becoming
And a seed is not an end, nor a means—
Every possible chaos is brought into being

For the appropriate potential to be achieved! And
Rather than arriving, I see starry movements,
Not aimless migrations, joining together day and night
Like overlapping maps! and for so long
Have we sought the sun-door through the circular stairs of dawn,
Yet, I behold as if its never been done,
Viewing with childlike paradisiac sight
To be edified with new illuminations, whilst simultaneously
Looking for home in the belly of the moon, courted by
A realm of questioning that shines with a borrowed light
Just as flowers, in their open-ended bargain, are
Exchanging light for breath (their language made of song)
Moving across the eternal moment with the stillness of an image
And a seed is a flower that has failed to notice it has died
Busily dreaming an ancient dream,
Nature's spontaneity leading the leash
An unceasingly renewed essence that the gods don't let decay

Rather than arriving, we will explore this open-endedness;
We wont ask what it means

Ecologists of the Inner Landscape

Let us become ecologists of the inner landscape, too: at times sitting immovably in one place, listening to the fervid bird calls of thought, watching as they wander like clouds that make no tracks. See how said thought and all such phenomenon dynamically relate to each other and move in circular paths like migratory butterflies—how time moves through thee in blossoming velocities to the seasons of your breath.

Note the lovely and terrible colors there, which the spring longingly displays; the fruits to be bore in thickets of thorns. Behold for a moment the invisible rivers of wind called emotion, And how no one really knows where they come from (nor where they're going). And, not least, those stormy urges of the heart: O those ineluctable night-blooming urges!

See the contours that the winter rain intimately reveals; the strangely familiar topographies that give shape to this land we briefly yet reverently call home. See where the frost gathers last and also where they melt first; that song of rain tapping with unseen fingers against roofs; and how no one really knows where this song ends: O how it sounds like a hundred doors opening in my mind at one time!

And now noticing those great currents of sunshine that pass over your mind's sky that both enchant and torment as it lights things unbeknownst to thee. And yet again, how no one really knows whence these currents come. But still: these mountainous vastnesses of possibility thus uncovered! Those tragically miraculous abysses over which our wings flutter covetously; how our intuition knows where life hides, and the giddy feeling of peering over precipices. And even more: O how a single breath can barely accommodate the vastness of your heart!

Let us come to know what persists indomitably in this landscape of veiled patterns, of seasons ever becoming. With nature as our mirror, let our eyes open upon the outer world, to find in it, continuity with our interior landscape, to find the movie screen telling the tale of our inner being, to notice the ecology of all objects, as if they formed constellations just for you to see. We have the means to subdue every beast of the wilderness, but no one can hide from what's behind their eyes. And O what dreadful joy to fall in love with that which is yet unmastered deep inside!

OPPOSITE OF A MOTH

Again and again I search through myself, and I am getting to know this labyrinthine castle called my soul: the marble archways, the bridges that lead to God knows where, the spires that rise to part the sky—and here there is so much sky; the dizzyingly rich faces hidden in the rock. Again and again I find in the fortress of my solitude a multitude of voices, but scarcely can I remember what these silent symphonies tell me: its hard to see this world as it is, in itself, as if looking into cavernous depths of sky. And I can't seem to look at it without wanting something more.

Shall it always be thus? How could I have not sought my outermost limit? What is the opposite of a moth? Roots that gladly reach into a farther darkness! O the obsession that verges upon curse! That suspends me by the hands of verdant canopies; that permits me a vision, to look through azure windows. Is it the divinity of human potential that torments me so? Am I just praying that my future will find me? But surely there are worse things than being forgotten among the flowers, among the wooden castles; worse things like addressing too many questions to the pure night sky.

Again and again I return to the worlds guileless simplicity; I will always walk across the rocky strands, between oceans of silence. And I think it is true: that you have to put the crown on your own head; that you have to find your own way through the labyrinthine castles. And yet, through this confusion awareness is expanded: and the dream of some lost paradise is a decadently fragile bridge I build—and there is still no name for where it actually leads me. Again and again it must be won, again and again I shall carry my blood,
even if everyday the answers change.
At last! and again I want to know my Self.

Song of My Longing

I

"Once, if I remember well, my life was a feast
where all hearts opened and all wines flowed."
-Arthur Rimbaud-

This incomprehensible riddle that I call my life
Made bearable only by love
Wearied by the weight of my name
The ghosts ever in tow
Nobody really gets away with anything
Or so I've been told

This beautiful folly that I call my life
Has grown huge as though rooted in honey
Some light must have gone through my lavender veins
To make my blood blossom in this way
And O how it gets me through the great waiting of winter
With unbearable delight & quiet exuberance

This absurd uncertainty that I call my life
Pardon me as I fall down vast rabbit holes
And make great mazes for myself
And get trapped within the castles of my mind:
Forgive me if I'm irrevocably mistaken
If I'm never quite sure, if this constant dying of ideas,
And subsequent endless reworking of thus,
Never amounts to more than a castle of dust

These vigilant actions I take to keep chaos at bay
And the short-lived but gorgeous order
That I call my life: once in a while

Some melodious harmony is strung together
—That music, I call that my meaning
O how I strive to utter each syllable
As if it's a brick building a great castle of song

And if perchance I'm successful
If my thought and word and action
Can form a bond with truth
Well then maybe that castle
Will be permitted to stand
For a spell

And this terrible paradox that I call my life
Can both transcend limitation
And exist within the tension
Juxtaposed and present together
Blessed be the balance struck thereof!
—That melody is when life makes sense
Or at least an intimation of it

II

*"But one day the 'why' arises and everything begins
in that weariness tinged with amazement."*
-Albert Camus-

The subtitles of my life
Seem to be written by a stranger
With foreign fingers in a disappearing ink
And today I cant seem to find my mind
Like a feral cat that wont come inside

Is it cause I want an echo of what's to come?
To get started on what can never be done
To let a thousand flowers bloom,

Save for me just a few crumbs

What other choice do we have in the matter
Than to become a door for the unbegotten, through which
What wants to become and what wants to be left behind
Can move as freely as a wind on trembling lips

But to where flows the gold of the rose?
The forever-vernal thirst that burns
If I knew I'd be the first to tell you
That's why I move longingly toward infinity
Beholden to the nostalgia for unity
Because I care about what's invisible
Because I don't like being burdened by obsolete maps
There are those things about which you cannot ask why
The lyrics of my thoughts inevitably arrive to the asking of why

My mind is prodded on by the manifold strangenesses
The narrative needs characters;
The drama needs props, needs obstacles
But who could know what it takes to live another's life?
Who could be absolutely sure that they're in touch with reality?
And that they're not too terribly fraught with paradox
And in wantonness squandered providence

Or become too dreadfully erroneous
While composing myths about futures hence
While trying to enhance the grandeur
And follow that one thread through it all:
That thread you see through it all?
That's your trail to walk: the path that blooms open for you
And only *you* can walk it
That seed that's always stuck in your teeth?
I call that potential; Yes: potential

Like all the possible songs that could erupt
Like a tumult of thunder from you
Like all that you find worth noticing
As though it shines with a peculiar radiance of meaning
Reading what is written into the topographies
Of your fingerprints
And you keep reaching out to grasp it
As a prize that stretches your fathoming ever further

Cause you can always get there from here
That thread you see through it all?
It's tied to you, even now
It's a wobbly rope we walk to get there
Within the flux of becoming
(Be not afraid of thy higher self)
That thing that's worth a lifetime of devotion?
Surely it's worthy of our worship
I call that potential; Yes: potential
It's a thing that's only yours,
That's never been seen on Earth before

To get there you need mirrors
For nothing can be hidden when everything is a mirror
And thus: can I ask you the questions
I really want to ask myself?
The ones only said in the presence of night
The ones only listened to by silence

I wish to ask those questions that get us into trouble
Those ones that make the politically correct panic
There are those things about which you cannot ask why
To learn of them requires proper sacrifice,
Requires an exploration of abysses within

Where dwells the chaos that gives birth to stars?

If you want to reach that place of which
Directions cannot be given
You must know there is a compass,
Must be willing to wrestle with riddles,
Must be like a spider that can catch
The most imperceptible thread
Seeking the link to your source
That you may live from your center
That you may turn the chaos of infinity into melody

What's worth noticing?
What's worthy of forgetting?
What then does the question become
When you've grown weary of every answer?

Am I my myth?
Or is my life an attempt at an answer, and hence a symbol?
These questions! how they tremble upon my lips

III

"Should not my longing overleap the distance
And draw the fairest form into existence?"
-Goethe's Faust-

There burns a vernal thirst in me
An unbearably ardent longing perpetually present
Not even a thousand winds could dry it

If only I could foresee
The fated day that would bring,
The inevitable coalescence to consummation,
To provide some modest consolation
Some slight assuaging

But would I dare glimpse that day?
In my folly would I venture to alleviate the inconsolable?
For I am its beast of burden; I kneel to bear it,
Bent within its tension my meaning is thereby derived
And thus the lion that fights for it,
And thus the child that gazes amazedly at it

You see: we long for its exalted fury
For nothing to be withheld, nothing unspent
No buffer from the danger
To be wrapped within the curl of its wave
And thereby commune with doom

For it is deadly in the best way
Like a beautiful woman, rising above mediocrity
It threatens to destroy what's dismal in us
We die by what we live by, do we not?
It does us well to be contrasted against magnificence
However terrifying it may be

For beauty is that which our longing dissolves into
The hardest of all attainment
Our desire for it be unappeasable
And I stumble towards the unutterable
As a blind man down dark hallways
Hopelessly groping, casting forth sound
In attempt to flesh out some vague features,
Some contour of the eternal face by sketching out the negative
space

Why can't I look away from those things that break my heart?
Those things that destroy *in order* to save you
Those things that make you swim away from shore
Into deep waters that can drown thee
Do small streams feel a fear of being drowned in a deeper sea?

Surely not: so let it be thus for me
What doesn't stay doesn't fear—what a tightrope act!
Becoming who you are is scary
But every drop is born to become ocean
To not find that confluence would be a fate much worse

Show me him whose eyes would
Be not scorched by such a vision!
And still I am the one who hunts for the location
Where the lightning will next strike
I may perish in the process, but I shall laugh at & love this fate
For in my perishing there's something that enlivens
Ah, blessed be what my blindness cannot foresee
Let it conspire to annihilate my cataclysmic ignorance
Let the veil of tears give way to an august vision

This is our redemption: to die when necessary
And O how this holy war imperils me
The intimate wildness that threatens with dissolution
The freedom that's realized by way of anguish
There is no guarantee of returning:
That's what makes it redemptive

And this is the confluence of truth and beauty:
The only safeguard against utter destruction
Is to ally thyself with the utmost truth you can muster
To establish a link between you and the divine principle
To bear the pain that truth might inflict
And for thus, art is the crucial healing balm

The aesthetic experience engenders a will to life
A salvation from the horrors;
The holy pain, as that of giving birth;
An innocent agony; to be synchronized
With the essence of the universe

And O how it calls out to us from beyond!
And our longing is that which calls back!
With magnificent agony, with great conflagrations

Indeed, it must be this very longing
That carries us across chasms of heart-haunting questions
That is like the lightning that bridges cloud to land
Thwarting the fear of having lived in vain
By compelling us to justify existence
Through our insatiable unrelenting expression of beauty
Even if it subjects us to melancholy
Could the quest for truth come at any less of a cost?
How could it be avoided?
This walking weighted on frail branches

My longing is the question I let echo
For its presence is more powerful than any answer
I long for something the world cannot give
The force of my yearning gives to the world
What the world cannot give to me

It is my compass
And I am the arrow aimed
I am its pillar of fire; my flesh,
Its scorchmark, its immolation;
A howling intensity within
Its sacrificial oblivion

THE FLOWER OF CHAOS

I

"That which you most need to see will be found
where you least want to look."
-Carl Jung-

All lost in a chaos
Mine was a calm apocalypse; a steady maelstrom
Set against the morning stars
With darkened eyes as coalmines

All fates to forsake, and I was bedamned!
Have you ever seen
The nightmare of your greatest fear
Unfold before your face?
& O how a curse would spread from my gaze

The taste of blood that's so often sought
Perchance to make peace with mortality
And we beckon to bear the rainweight
To wear the tempest's countenance on our brow
The underlying urge to breach our firewall
Cause everyone's got something to burn
For the baggage we carry is like kindling
Waiting for a wildfire

So I took, with immeasurable foolhardiness,
The prophet's pledge; the shaman's lone exile
Hastening to render the philosopher's stone
From the substance of my soul
Through the smoke of oracles & a screaming storm
To enter the deathly forest where it seemed to be darkest
Fascinated by what's forbidden

Seeking to find love's visionary company
Amid the black chasms of an inferno
& O how the midnight cried!

Of nails driven into me, the crucified mind
And the fractured snowflake melts
In the midst the searing ravines
Of hospital beds and tranquilizers wrestled,
Into my veins injecting
The black widow's webs were pulled in on me
& O how none could calm my fright, nor allay my palpitations

But what could splinter the immortal Soul?
That rests like a silent eye centered in the cycling tornadic
That withholds for the promise of old

II

*"And if thou gaze long into an abyss,
the abyss will also gaze into thee."*
-Friedrich Nietzsche-

All lost in an existentialist confusion
I had all but forgotten my name
And I didn't think you could come back from that
This penchant for going past the precipice edge
Into the chaos of the deepest abyss

Have you ever gone farther
Than your mind can fathom?
And then further still, past any return
(The only return being to go through,
And make the round of the great wheel)

Over five sleepless days and nights

O' the tricks of light!
O' the deceptions of shadow!
How the paranoia becomes more than one can bear
And your consciousness starts leaking out everywhere
Objects start malfunctioning;
Situations begin erupting all around
The structure of reality shaking apart
The container breaking—O' how I fell inside myself!

Is it a mental projection? Is it real or not?
Is this some world of daydreams?
Is it the same chaos God wrestled with at the beginning of time?
The same chaos He made the world out of?
Was it the farthermost distance from God,
That which we call hell?

How I had questioned everything
Till I no longer had a plank to walk upon,
Till the point of forgetfulness of what reality even is
When reality and dream get crossed up
And you're hung there in between
When the rug is pulled out from under you
One thread at a time—
All the makings of a fall from Grace
O' how I fell inside myself!

The submerged and feeble resolution of resignation
To stay inside yourself—catatonically
And then there is nothing left
But crippling fear of certain, imminent death
Spiraling into nightmare, embattled
Harrowed in the throes of Hell
Was I invited into a minefield?

Or was this Chaos a potential not yet tamed?

(But you have to be able to see in the dark)
I was being invited to sacrifice
Who I perceived & believed myself to be
I was being invited to die
That I may witness the sacred design
And move toward wholeness

III

"We must learn to die: that is all of life."
-Rainer Maria Rilke-

Have you ever been so lost
You thought there was no hope for being found?
Lost in your own irony
O' the comfortable certainties collapsing into complexity!
And what could be more complicated than a human being?
Our inexhaustible ability to render meaning
And what could be more powerful than the mind?
To generate and project hallucinated perception
Onto the external screen of being

If you see the face of chaos then you've gone too far
(Or maybe I had finally made it?)
I saw the face of chaos
And what level of hell did I find myself in?
The fourth floor mental health ward
The strangest stage for rebirth & initiation
Sunken so low I hit the archetypal substructures
The place from where all patterns arise
And how then the senses felt like an affliction

But I saw it all:
Where the pariahs go to die
Or at least submit surrender—but what's the difference?

174

Scribbling in bibles; theirs was a chaos barely inhabitable
The pattern of *pills, meal, therapy* on repeat
Was not enough to bring them back
Looking out from a fourth floor window
They who go months without sweet air on bare skin
No stars in sight to chart a course
Past, present and future all bleeding together
"Did I ever really know myself?"
The thoughts resound in an echo chamber

Was mine a divine injunction
That made me relinquish my intransigence?
The holy fear to precede the holy joy
The pitch of madness tinged with religious implication
And mythological allusion
It was a different kind of real
For which coherence was sacrificed
To be baptized in a bath of shadows
To retrieve from the suffocated ocean depths of my psyche
My reason for being, and you cannot get to the gold
Without facing the dragon or going inside the whale
That much is certain

But their eyes seemed to say:
"Is this your first time dying?"
Its as if their far-off stare
Endeavors to make you never forget
This place of exile, vast and vacant
Dalliances with delusional divine chaos
O the ineffable lamentations of the damned
Unbearably fragile mind—what is real?
Hast thou forsaken me?

I saw the shadow that can't be unseen
And it was my own

If you stare long enough into the darkness
It will reveal what you least want to see
The hell within myself had externalized
Into the raw nakedness of chaos
Stripped down to the soul

But could I see paradise if it was right in front of me?
Was it the Kingdom of Heaven I was stumbling toward all along?
Longing to see that which is inescapably true—
Or was I all long being chased
By that which is inescapably true?
Had I reached that fated dead end?
Where the only choices were
To be irretrievably lost

The underlying satire of cosmic intervention:
I begin to bargain with God
Trying to call in every favor
Am I the sacrifice of sweet savor?
Acquiescing to my trial
All too guilty of uninitiated egotism,
Fearful of the abyss within, lacking any kind of instruction
On how one is to wander through a dark cruel ocean

And hospital attendees seemed to be dark legions
Bent on the fatal imprisonment of the damned
Their faces both caustic and menacing
Mirroring my freight
Conspiring in favor of my demise
Herding along the funeral procession

Catatonia, psychosis, depression, bipolar, schizophreniform,
& O how grandiose a delusion
—The psyche's only possible response
To the overwhelm of terror and chaos,

To the ultimate sacred defeat
Of my little isle flooded by the Greater Being
For I had hooked a fish that was bigger than I
And didn't know how to let go

How was I to know that the shadow with which I wrestle
Is a being whose dimensions are impossible to measure?
And the crushing weight of irreducible questions
I could almost see the face I had
Before I was born

But the official remedy for such cases is an even greater insanity,
A pill each: one anti-psychotic, one anti-depressant,
One anti-anxiety, one for inducing sleep, and then one for
Combating the possible side effects
Of the whole terrible pharmaceutical onslaught
But at least it made me sleep!

IV

*"And to die is different from what anyone supposed,
and luckier."*
-Walt Whitman-

All lost with purpose
Like when you find the exact amount of change
In your pocket that you need
As if every moment is a directive
Handed directly to you from the Most High
But beware of unearned wisdom!
Time will certainly catch up with you
And when it does the scales will be balanced

There is no amount of impassioned hyperbole
That can make another understand the self-annihilation

And even if I did tell you, would you believe me?
That my universe went dark
Right there in the middle of summer
That my deluded visions
Saw only the certain apocalypse, the terminus of "me"
O the multitudinous meanings to be seen
O the perilous fragility of this moment

But finding *your* meaning
Is the heroic antidote to life's endless vicissitudes
Inexorably, you will be pilloried
But don't be an unaccounted variable in a flawed equation
Lest you become a parody of yourself
The shallow moors that get swept by storms
Things that only a fool could conjure
And yet, O the floods I wept!

It could be that I was touched with the firebrands
And tickled by the golden feathers of the firebird
To retrieve the smoking souvenir
Trying to imagine that which
Only a madman could fathom
One foot ever-further into the unfamiliar
Efforting to bargain with the future
The self-immolation—of when a forest
Has went too long unburned

Or did You take one
Of your blessed feathers
And waft an innocuous whisper in my ear?
Thus to make me, for a moment,
Forget my name, that I may remember
The supernal meaning of being
Or at least bear the burden of being
In a heroic manner

Or have I masqueraded
Under the guise of virtue (an anathema to truth)
Playing a trick on myself?
Caught at the crossroads in the desert where devils dwell
In the underworld where the dragons slumber
And the cherubim's wielding flame
Keeping me from the gardens of youth

I was tempted to look away
Upon realizing that I'm not what I could be
The initial inclination is to hide, and that may be appropriate,
Its likely way worse than you thought
But you are much greater than you think
You have the power to get the snakes out of your garden
And disabuse yourself of illusory notions,
To make the devil explain himself
To tussle with God

Forget not who you were yesterday
And all the years, they may have carried you here
But now is as good of time as any
To let yourself die unto the unbeknownst
Lest it keep you from becoming who you actually are

Who you are is that which has to be sacrificed
For who you must become
Who you momentarily thought you were
Was provisional—a guiding post
The painting doesn't end at the frame
Your true identity dwells deeper—
A ground you can stand on
And from there you can actually aim for
Your own approximation of heaven

That's not to say that one should betray the former self
But even if there's nothing left but a husk
You must empty thy cup
For how many branches in your forest are held up
Only by the grip of splinters waiting for the weight of rain?
Bear your name to time and see what is actually edified
Because there are worse things than dying
It will be touch and go
But what could break the indestructible Soul?

V

"Finally I came to regard as sacred
the disorder of my mind."
-Arthur Rimbaud-

Then I let the vagaries of fate
Aid my wakefulness and humility
Even if they may be punctuated by catastrophe
It's the flailing that makes you drown faster
Is there such a thing as waking up gracefully?

Some flowers open in a storm,
Some seeds are coaxed open when caressed by flame
And, having been beyond the brink,
The *katabasis* is the soul's seed bank
Where chaos is wrestled into ripened potential
O night-blooming one!
The brightest blossoms spring from a darkest abyss
Where shadowy turbid fertility collects

There we find the imperishable rose ungathered
And from such a chaos we fashion an ark
That takes us to a new world,
And from such a chaos we *build* the new world:

Chaos is that art not yet rendered,
Gathered from the darkest night

O theft of the undying fire!
Slipped into abysses, beset with oblivion
What is better than having a problem
That's really worth solving? —The conundrum of existence
To rage against the move toward meaninglessness:
The onus is ours
That which gives your life the ultimate contrast
Is a rock bottom to which you can never go back

The fear best faced head on
Lest you ignore it at your compounded peril
Lest it come find you on its own terms
Increased into tragedy —That's when tragedy turns into hell
The experience of which is rightly called nightmare

A flood will surely come; the end is ever nigh
But you will win out
For your potential is proportionate to
The chaos that you encounter

For you *are* the Flower of Chaos!
Eternally emerging forth from beyond belief
Beyond the limits of perception
The realm of religious experience
Is often coincident with a temporary break
From consensual reality
The place where chaos is wildcrafted and danced with
Where cosmos is composed

It is a wilderness from which *you* are wrought
To shepherd the supernal seeds
Through life's ephemeral fragility

Allied with enamored grace and triumphant restraint
—Is this not the message of any flower?

Your every act has redemptive capacity
Vindicate all beings by your alignment
To the true structure of reality
By walking the strait path
And this ripple will move unto others

And the whole Cosmos of Being shall be ameliorated
The force that flows from you is your choosing
Despite your perceived inadequacies
Despite your lingering sense of shame
An overwhelming force of good can be unleashed
From the deeps of your being

Persist! In the face of your lamentable ignorance
Leap! Into the once-inconceivable
Let your body be the bridge
For all that's unbridgeable!
Let your words exceed the limits of silence!

For you can breathe through anything
For your very breath is the force of God
Brought forth into existence
The very means by which the Divine
Makes love with you through the world

To sacrifice your life to the Most High
The prerequisite is to be laid low, lower than low
The corollary is to posit the ultimate aim
And open your door to it
This initiation becomes your life's touchstone
Calibrating the compass & giving the arrow its thrust
For the bottom is just the beginning

There are songs that await thee; there are seasons yet promised

Because time cannot expire the imperishable soul!
Outlasting tragedy, unable to be eclipsed
By the forsakenness of existence
Outlasting every kingdom, the countless thousand-year voyage
Of leaving nothing unnamed amidst the great drama of Being
There is no doubt you will die, but can you live in a way
That justifies dying? Dare to discover your answer

Dare to love your fate:
That life would give to you its utmost opposition and obstacle,
That it would *make* you find your will to rise,
After being unwittingly led into your depths,
That it would trust you with the greatest tragedy
Is reason all the more to bless your suffering
Like you bless your happiness
To praise it through the abundance of your being

By cultivating victory from the forlornness
By climbing back from the darkest abyss
With some petals of the sun, singing your soul's song
What you found there is for everyone
You are *because* you belong
It is *you* that the world has asked for
And every action becomes an offering
As you discover the dream that's been dreaming you all along
And lend your myth to God

* * *

www.ingramcontent.com/pod-product-compliance
Lightning Source LLC
Chambersburg PA
CBHW031329060726
47590CB00012B/2309